Embracing Empathy in Healthcare

A UNIVERSAL APPROACH TO PERSON-CENTRED, EMPATHIC HEALTHCARE ENCOUNTERS

ANNEMIEKE P BIKKER

Researcher
Institute of Health and Wellbeing, University of Glasgow

PHILIP COTTON

General Practitioner
Principal, College of Medicine and Health Sciences, University of Rwanda
Professor of Learning and Teaching, University of Glasgow

STEWART W MERCER

General Practitioner
Professor of Primary Care Research, University of Glasgow
National Lead for Multimorbidity Research, Scottish School of Primary Care

Radcliffe Publishing
London • New York

Radcliffe Publishing Ltd
St Mark's House
Shepherdess Walk
London N1 7BQ
United Kingdom

www.radcliffehealth.com

British Library Cataloguing in Publication Data

A catalogue record for this book is available from the British Library.

ISBN-13: 978 190936 818 7

The paper used for the text pages of this book
is FSC® certified. FSC (The Forest Stewardship
Council®) is an international network to promote
responsible management of the world's forests.

Typeset by Darkriver Design, Auckland, New Zealand
Printed and bound by Hobbs the Printers, Totton, Hants, UK

Contents

About the authors

The CARE Approach was developed at the University of Glasgow, Scotland.

Annemieke Bikker is a researcher in the Institute of Health and Wellbeing at the University of Glasgow, and has previously researched practitioner–patient interactions, verbal and non-verbal communication and their links to health outcomes

Philip Cotton is a general practitioner and Principal of the College of Medicine and Health Sciences at the University of Rwanda. He is professor of learning and teaching at the University of Glasgow.

Stewart Mercer is a general practitioner and professor of primary care research in the Institute of Health and Wellbeing at the University of Glasgow. He is the national lead for multimorbidity research with the Scottish School of Primary Care. He is internationally recognised for his research on the clinical encounter and the needs of patients with complex conditions. A full list of Stewart's publications and current research can be found at: www.gla.ac.uk/researchinstitutes/healthwellbeing/staff/stewartmercer/#tabs=1

Acknowledgements

The following actors and practitioners feature in the clips:
- Paddy Bonner, actor
- Alicia Devine, actress
- Pene Herman-Smith, actress
- Sarah McCardie, actress
- Philip Cotton, general practitioner
- Fiona McNeney, physiotherapist
- Stewart Mercer, general practitioner
- Karen Pirie, podiatrist

The clips were made at the Media Production Unit at the University of Glasgow. The development of the CARE Approach was sponsored by the Self-Management Programme of the Long Term Conditions Unit, The Scottish Government.

Introduction

WELCOME TO THE CARE APPROACH

Conversations between patients and practitioners lie at the very heart of healthcare. Such conversations happen day in and day out in primary care clinics and hospitals, when patients consult their general practitioner (GP), attend an outpatient appointment, see their physiotherapist or visit their practice nurse for a minor illness or chronic disease management. The list of opportunities for healthcare conversations is almost endless given the wide range of staff working in modern healthcare systems and the different ways in which encounters can happen. In the course of a career, a healthcare professional is likely to have hundreds of thousands of clinical encounters.

Although these encounters may at times be quite straightforward, the days when the healthcare professional simply imparted technical expertise and knowledge to a receptive and passive patient are long gone. In today's world, patients and carers expect to be engaged in a partnership with practitioners in their healthcare and wish to be informed about and involved in decisions. The encounter can be a complex phenomenon, where both parties bring expertise and knowledge and engage in a conversation about a certain problem or set of problems. The hallmark of high-quality healthcare is responding effectively to the needs of each individual patient, and good communication between practitioner and patient is a key part of this.

To be an effective healthcare practitioner therefore requires mastery of not only the technical aspects of care but also of the human aspects (Campbell *et al.*, 2000). Research has consistently shown that patients rate empathic communication and patient-centredness as top priorities (Stewart *et al.*, 2003; Wensing *et al.*, 1998; Little *et al.*, 2000; Mercer & Reynolds, 2002; Mercer *et al.*, 2004, 2007). Training can improve both clinical empathy (Mercer & Reynolds 2002; Reiss *et al.*, 2012; Batt-Rawden *et al.*, 2013) and patient-centredness (Dwamena *et al.*, 2012). Empathic, patient-centred care improves health outcomes (Little *et al.*, 2001; Griffin *et al.*, 2004; Bikker *et al.*, 2005; Mercer *et al.*, 2008; Derkson *et al.*, 2013). This applies to both acute (Rakel *et al.*, 2011) and chronic (Hojat *et al.*, 2011) conditions.

Maintaining or improving empathic communication in healthcare practitioners is important, since several studies have shown that empathy tends to decline over time (Neumann *et al.*, 2011). Clearly this has direct implications for patients' health

1

outcomes, as well as for patients' satisfaction (Neumann *et al.*, 2009) and enablement (Mercer *et al.*, 2002; Mercer *et al.*, 2012).

The CARE Approach focuses on these human aspects of care. Also, how the words are used and non-verbal cues, as well as responses to these, are vitally important in creating encounters that are satisfying and enabling (Bikker *et al.*, 2013). The CARE Approach aims to assist you in developing, practising and reflecting on empathic, person-centred communication, and this book is a practical tool to help you in this endeavour. We hope the CARE Approach will inspire and support you in the encounters you have with the people you care for in your work – that is, your patients. However, you may even find the CARE Approach helps you in your interactions with colleagues and friends.

WHAT IS THE CARE APPROACH?

The 'CARE Approach' is a framework for empathic, person-centred encounters in healthcare interactions. It is derived from the Consultation and Relational Empathy, (CARE) Measure (*see* Appendix 1), which is a widely used patient-rated measure of the clinical encounter. Whereas the CARE Measure is used to measure patients' experiences of the interpersonal aspects of clinical encounters, the CARE Approach has been specifically developed to help practitioners reflect on, practise, maintain and improve their communication skills and to use these skills effectively in helping to empower and enable the patient. This learning resource has been developed for use by a wide range of healthcare practitioners. It can be used by individuals, groups and organisations. The CARE Approach can be used in combination with the CARE Measure or as a stand-alone learning tool.

The CARE Measure (and thus the CARE Approach) is based on a broad definition of 'relational empathy' in the clinical context, which is defined as the ability to:
- understand the patient's situation, perspective and feelings (and their attached meanings)
- communicate that understanding and check its accuracy; and
- act on that understanding with the patient in a helpful (therapeutic) way (Reynolds, 2000; Mercer & Reynolds, 2002).

The CARE Approach has four interacting components:

Connecting

Assessing

Responding

Empowering

The ways in which the CARE Approach components broadly map onto the ten items that make up the CARE Measure are shown in Table 1. The table also outlines aspects of the practitioners' interpersonal skills that relate most to each of the CARE

Approach components. The key principle underlying the CARE Approach is flexibility. Each encounter is unique – it has never happened before and it will never happen again – and thus it requires awareness, sensitivity, an unconditional acceptance of the patient and of his or her needs, and an ability to be present and respond in the moment. It is also influenced by context. For example, what may be helpful and appropriate in an in-depth psychiatric assessment may not be so in an exchange between a healthcare assistant and a patient attending to have a blood sample taken. As such, the CARE Approach is not intended to be a rigid set of rules to be applied in the same way in every encounter, but rather a broad set of guiding principles to be applied flexibly according to the situation and circumstance.

TABLE 1 Overview of the CARE Approach components in relation to the CARE Measure

CARE Approach component	Description of component in relation to practitioners' interpersonal skills	CARE Measure items that CARE Approach component maps onto (each is rated by the patient)
Connecting	Actively engaging with the patient to create or deepen rapport and to facilitate open communication within a safe 'environment'	1. Making you feel at ease 2. Letting you tell your story
Assessing	Listening and taking a holistic approach to fully understand the patient's situation, perspective and feelings (and their attached meanings)	3. Really listening 4. Being interested in you as a whole person 5. Fully understanding your concerns
Responding	Communicating your understanding (and checking its accuracy) in a caring and compassionate way, responding positively with clear explanations if appropriate	6. Showing care and compassion 7. Being positive 8. Explaining things clearly
Empowering	Helping the patient to feel more in control according to their abilities, preferences and values, and planning their treatment in partnership with them	9. Helping you take control 10. Making a plan of action with you

STRUCTURE OF THE LEARNING TOOL

The CARE Approach learning tool consists of eight modules, with each module building on the one before.
- Module 1 is about the attitudes, beliefs and values you (as a person) bring to each encounter.
- Modules 2, 3, 4 and 5 address the four components of the CARE Approach, describing the key aspects of each and explaining how each component operates and can be applied and developed in practice.

- Module 6 is about 'putting all the components together' and demonstrating the CARE Approach in action. It is about the spirit of the CARE Approach.
- Module 7 examines the CARE Approach in the context of teamwork.
- Module 8 concerns the facilitation of the CARE Approach.

For ease of explanation and understanding, the CARE Approach components are separated and presented in sequence. However, it will quickly become apparent that 'Connecting', for example, is not necessarily an exclusive domain of the start of an encounter, and the practitioner and patient can connect and reconnect (perhaps deepening the connection) many times during a single encounter or through successive encounters.

Throughout the modules, suggested exercises, audio recordings and video clips of patient–practitioner encounters are included to illustrate certain points, facilitate learning and reflection, and help you respond in relation to your own working environment. The clips of the encounters are simulated and show interactions between actor-patients and real healthcare practitioners. A worksheet on which to record your answers is provided within this book (*see* 'The CARE Approach worksheet'). Possible answers to the exercises are included for modules 1 to 6. Additional information on the background of the CARE Approach can be found in Appendix 4.

Please note that in this book we refer to the patient interchangeably as 'he' or 'she'.

The video clips and audio recordings are available at
www.radcliffehealth.com/empathy

MODULES

MODULE 1: What you bring to the encounter

This module explores:
- what 'caring' means to you
- the difference between patient-oriented and disease- or task-oriented encounters
- the importance of both verbal and non-verbal communication
- the ways in which your attitudes, beliefs and values influence the encounter.

CARING

'Caring' is an emotive term and people interpret the word in different ways.

Exercise 1.1

1. What is your response to the word 'caring'? What thoughts come to mind? What feelings do you associate with the word? (*See* 'Possible answers', p. 119.)
2. What are the aspects of your job that make it possible for you to practise in ways that you consider to be caring?

PATIENT-ORIENTED VERSUS DISEASE- OR TASK-ORIENTED ENCOUNTERS

In a 'patient-oriented' encounter, the healthcare professional creates opportunities for the patient to express his views, concerns, beliefs and priorities regarding his care, and to participate as fully as he wishes to in the decision-making process. To put it another way, a patient-oriented encounter is about realising that the patient is at the centre of care, and as healthcare professionals our task is to work effectively in partnership with the person, and at times, his family members and carers.

In contrast, in a 'task-oriented' encounter, the healthcare professional completes a series of tasks that 'need to be done to the patient' in the time given and the agenda is driven by the structures and processes of the healthcare system. The tasks are relevant to the patient, but the patient's views, concerns, beliefs and priorities are set aside by the need to 'get the job done'. In this case, it is the practitioner's (or the system's) needs that take priority and are reflected in her behaviour, attitude, and verbal and non-verbal communication. Similarly, a 'disease-oriented encounter' focuses on the patient's illness rather than the whole person. The patient is seen as the 'diabetic in bed 3' rather than the 'person in bed 3 who has diabetes', for whom, in fact, the disease might not be the major concern at that time.

If we are used to a task- or disease-oriented approach in the patient–practitioner encounter, we may also be used to 'telling' a patient what to do without making sure that she understands the advice, whether she is motivated to follow the advice and what worries she has. The task-oriented approach may reflect how we have been trained, what we have learned from others, and the structures and processes within the workplace. In task-oriented encounters, we drive the interaction with the patient and can choose to cover only those things we feel we have time for or the ability to deal with.

Exercise 1.2

The following exercise is designed to raise your awareness of whether you communicate in a patient-oriented or in a disease- or task-oriented manner.

1. What features best characterise you when interacting with a patient. For example, do you tend to reassure, listen well or take control?
2. Consider the types of patient interactions you have. List situations when you are most likely to be patient oriented and when are you most likely to be task or disease oriented.
3. For each of the situations you have listed in 2, describe whether you are aiming to meet your own needs or the patient's needs.

Moving to a more patient-oriented approach may involve going beyond the way we conduct our encounters with patients. While this may sound daunting, depending on the context, this can often be achieved through small changes, such as making appropriate eye contact, smiling, listening more and talking less, checking that you have understood the patient's concerns and sharing decisions with the patient about the plan of action ahead. In a nutshell, it is about paying attention to the patient who has come to you for help as an individual, and responding to them in a helpful and non-patronising way.

Exercise 1.3

1. Think of yourself as a patient. What would the ideal doctor or nurse be like and how would they behave towards you?

Record your answers on the worksheet.

(*See* 'Possible answers', p. 119.)

2. In what ways are these behaviours important? (*See* 'Possible answers', p. 119.)

COMMUNICATION

Communication is central to the CARE Approach. The way we express ourselves has a direct effect on those around us. Effective communication needs good verbal and non-verbal skills. In broad terms, 'verbal communication' relates to what is said while 'non-verbal communication' refers to how something is said. Thus, non-verbal communication includes the tone and speed of speech as well as body language, such as eye contact, facial expressions and posture. We tend to be less aware of our own non-verbal behaviour than our verbal communication, as it happens subconsciously. Yet our non-verbal communication powerfully 'speaks' to the other person, conveying our attitudes and feelings. Our non-verbal behaviour plays a much bigger part in overall communication than we realise and can facilitate or hinder the effectiveness of what we are saying. When *what* is said contradicts *how* it is said, people tend to believe the non-verbal message. For example, a patient is less likely to be convinced that you are really listening to them, even if you say so, if you persist in looking at the computer screen. Therefore, for our message to be effective and credible, it is important that we match what we say and how we say it.

VALUES AND BELIEFS

'Values' relate to beliefs about what is right and wrong, what you consider important and what you think should be done in certain circumstances. Values relate to how we view and understand the world and they give meaning to what we do in life. They underpin our attitudes (assumptions, expectations and judgements), behaviour and the way we communicate. Therefore, it is important to be aware of the values, beliefs and attitudes that we hold, and thus what we bring (consciously or not) to the encounter.

We are not born with values and beliefs. We develop them as we grow and mature, through our parenting, our education and our interactions with others. Like all things in life, they can change. Conflicts can arise when our values and behaviour do not correspond, or when we are working in an environment that is at odds with our values or does not allow us to express them. Our values may also 'leak' through our communication in a way that patients find unhelpful, prejudicial, judgemental and confusing.

Exercise 1.4

This exercise is called the 'respected figures' exercise.
1. In the first column, write down the names of at least two and up to five people who you deeply respect for the way they have led or lead their lives. You do not have to respect everything about them, but in one or more significant ways, you should admire how they have or do live. These people could be living or dead, famous or not famous, known to you personally or simply heard about.

(*continued over*)

2. In the second column, write down the qualities they had or have that you respect. What is it about them that you admire? Then look for individual qualities or clusters of qualities that stand out. A particular quality may stand out simply because you know inside that it is of great importance to you, or because the same quality appears next to more than one person on the chart – possibly described in a slightly different way.

3. Write down up to three such qualities in the third column. If you are not being overly idealistic, these qualities are likely to represent *root* values, which are crucially important for you to try to live by.

Who do you deeply respect for the way they have led/lead their life?	What are the qualities this person had/has that you particularly respect?	What are the three key qualities this person had/has that you particularly respect?
1.		
2.		
3.		
4.		
5.		

From Hawkins (2013). Permission obtained from Dr James Hawkins.

DO YOU LIVE YOUR VALUES?

Consider the values you have identified in Exercise 1.4, the respected figures task. Do you live these values yourself? In what ways do you try to live these values in your personal and professional life? What are the things that help you bring these values into your everyday life? What are the things that prevent this from happening?

Exercise 1.5

Make a list of your top three root values, and consider the questions in the previous paragraph. Can you make any changes in your work or personal life that would allow you to live your values more fully?

MODULE 2: Connecting

CARE

This module explores:
- the importance of 'connecting' in the encounter
- how to enhance your rapport with your patients
- how to make effective use of non-verbal communication
- how to encourage the 'patient narrative' as part of connecting.

'Connecting' is what happens when you 'click' with someone. It often occurs naturally and spontaneously between two people when they first meet and very quickly like each other. As this occurs at a subconscious level, it can be difficult to describe exactly why it has happened. When it happens, we just know it and it feels good! We can also sense its absence when it does not happen (and it can create a mutual feeling of unease). You probably have examples in which you remember feeling how easily you connected with someone, without being able to put into words why.

Of course, connecting is a two-way process and as such it cannot be forced or faked. However, in the CARE Approach, we suggest that connecting is a key component of the patient encounter and thus in your professional role you may need to work at maximising the chances of connecting with your patient. Fortunately, you can learn to optimise connecting, which for the healthcare professional is an active process that requires both conscious effort and willingness (Neighbour, 1987).

Within the context of the CARE Approach, 'connecting' refers to the start of the process of actively engaging with the patient. So patients will share their views and concerns with us, we need to do our best to ensure that they feel comfortable and at ease about doing so. Connecting covers four features that are part of empathic, person-centred communication. These are:

1. establishing rapport
2. accepting the patient as a person
3. effective non-verbal communication
4. allowing the patient to tell his or her 'story'.

ESTABLISHING RAPPORT

The process of establishing rapport involves creating a trusting atmosphere in which the patient feels comfortable to share personal information (Arnold & Boggs, 2007).

Establishing rapport starts at the very beginning of the encounter, for example, in the way we greet the patient in the waiting room and invite him to join us in the consulting room, or in the way we approach him at the bedside.

First impressions are important. The way we introduce ourselves (verbally and non-verbally) and our opening words and sentences form an essential part of connecting.

Exercise 2.1

View the clips showing different approaches then answer the following question. In what ways do the healthcare practitioners create a good first impression with the patients?

Clip 1

Clip 2

Clip 3

(See 'Possible answers', p. 120.)

ACCEPTING THE PATIENT AS A PERSON

We may not necessarily condone or approve of everything that the patient tells us, but accepting patients without prejudice is fundamental to an empathic approach. It demonstrates our respect for them and this facilitates connecting.

Although it may sound straightforward, interacting with people without making prejudicial judgements and treating them in a way that is equal and fair can be a challenge, because we can have tendencies to prefer certain types of people over others. Raising an eyebrow, making less eye contact or beginning to talk a touch more loudly are types of non-verbal behaviour that may be perceived as 'frosty' and could suggest that we are being critical (Davis, 2006).

Exercise 2.2

1. How easy or difficult would it be for you to accept and not judge the following people? Tick the box that most closely reflects your viewpoint.

	Very easy	Easy	Difficult	Very difficult	Impossible
1. A mother who does not control her disruptive child whose behaviour prevents you from understanding the mother's story					
2. A man who does not follow your advice and complains about the same issues over and over again					
3. A patient who blames you for her troubles					
4. A man who refuses to take any responsibility for his health and wants you to tell him exactly what to do					
5. A patient who demands your help in an aggressive manner					
6. A patient who talks and talks, but not about his health					
7. A woman who keeps taking over the conversation and does not listen to you					

2. Look at the people you have ticked as 'difficult', 'very difficult' or 'impossible'. What are some of the reasons for these answers?
3. In what healthcare situations have you had to set aside personal biases, values and judgements?

Exercise 2.3

Read the following remarks made by patients who took part in a study on quality in general practice consultations in Glasgow, Scotland (Mercer *et al.*, 2007). Reflect on what you think the patients reacted to.

A. 'Some of them make you feel inadequate, you know you're getting old and you're getting senile and you're not able to take things in, I mean sometimes you feel that way, you feel as if oh I'll just lift my bag and jacket and go.'

B. 'I've got Dr X and Dr Y and the two of them have got totally different attitudes when it comes to talking to you, Dr X will take the time and listen to you.'

C. 'You feel as if you're taking up his [the doctor's] time . . . that makes you feel under pressure.'

D. 'When I go to see my doctor, I want him to see me, the person, not a bottle of methadone, I'm not that, I'm a person that's got needs and everything like everybody else, because I'm on methadone, I just don't get treated properly.'

(*See* 'Possible answers', p. 120.)

Quotes reproduced courtesy of BioMed Central.

EFFECTIVE NON-VERBAL COMMUNICATION

By now it should be clear that our non-verbal communication plays a big part in connecting with patients. It determines how we come across in our introduction and hence how approachable, trustworthy, accepting and interested we are perceived to be (Cole & Bird, 2000). Our non-verbal behaviour is especially important in communicating that we are listening. Here are a few simple pointers on non-verbal forms of communication that will aid the process of connecting.

- *Eye contact*: Appropriate eye contact is crucial. Prolonged eye contact may come across as 'staring' and patients may feel embarrassed or intimidated. Conversely, too little eye contact may come across as rather cold and patients may feel that you are not interested in what they are saying. If possible, it is important to be at eye level with the patient; for example, by having a chair that is the same height as the patient's.

- *Posture*: For very good reasons, the patient's chair is normally stable with four legs while the practitioner's chair is often a swivel seat on wheels. The practitioner has to complete various tasks and has to face the patient and the computer at different times during the encounter. Patients are more likely to perceive that the healthcare practitioner is interested and listening if they are sitting upright and leaning slightly forward than if the practitioner is slouching back in the chair. If we sit with our legs uncrossed and our arms unfolded, patients may be more likely to feel we are listening to them than if we sit with our legs crossed and our arms folded.

- *Signalling*: Achieving a balance between facing the patient and performing the tasks necessary to record information is important. Some practitioners find it useful to tell the patient what they are typing into the computer as they do this: 'Right, let me record this in your notes . . . you have had this pain for 4 weeks now . . .' and 'I am typing a note here to say that you should come back in 2 weeks if this doesn't clear up.' Practitioners also confirm that they are listening by occasionally saying things such as 'uh-uh' while using the computer.
- *Gestures and expressions*: Our gestures, like our seated posture, can make the difference between a patient feeling that she is being listened to or not. Our arm and hand movements and our facial expressions must match the content of what we say and what we hear. This is sometimes termed 'congruence'.
- *Voice inflection*: We can use the sound, speed and volume of our voice to communicate interest and warmth. Inappropriate use of our voice can (unintentionally) convey distance and coldness.

Exercise 2.4

View the clips. These versions of the clips have the sound removed. Watch these silent versions then answer the following question.

Clip 1 (without sound)

Clip 2 (without sound)

In what ways are the practitioners' non-verbal approaches to the patients different? If you wish, you can view the clips again with sound.

Clip 1 (with sound)

Clip 2 (with sound)

(*See* 'Possible answers', p. 120.)

ALLOWING THE PATIENT TO TELL HIS OR HER 'STORY'

People need time and space, and our attention, to fully describe their illness and concerns in their own way. Giving time and attention shows respect and interest. Ultimately, we want to obtain an understanding of what is on the person's mind and how he feels. After opening the encounter and inviting the patient to tell his story, we can encourage and facilitate storytelling by looking at the patient, nodding and by verbal utterances such as, 'uh-uh', 'okay' and 'really'.

There are many different reasons for encounters; for example, to monitor an illness or disease, to undergo a test or because there is a new symptom. However, it may be important to give patients the opportunity to tell us whatever they feel they need to, whatever their reason for coming to see us. Neutral, open, inviting questions are best. Here are a few examples of ways to invite patients to tell their story:

- 'How are you today?'
- 'What has happened since we last met?''
- Can you tell me a bit about the story of your back? Like when it started and how you ended up at physiotherapy today?'

Exercise 2.5

View the clip then answer the following question.

In what ways are the different aspects of connecting demonstrated in the clip? (The four aspects are: establishing rapport, accepting the patient as a person, effective non-verbal communication, allowing the patient to tell his or her story.)

(*See* 'Possible answers', p. 120.)

A FINAL WORD ON CONNECTING

Connecting is a thread that runs through the whole encounter and is not confined to the first few minutes. Opportunities for connecting may develop and deepen over time, either within a single encounter or over a series of encounters. In some branches of healthcare, such as primary care, general practice, mental health and the care of older people, continuity of care is both possible and desirable, and allows you and the patient to work together over time. The more we connect with a patient, and re-establish and reinforce the connection, the stronger the therapeutic relationship will be. Here are some examples of phrases you can use to make connections over time:

- 'I remember you telling me about . . .'
- 'How is your daughter these days?'
- 'You mentioned that a while back, tell me more . . .'
- 'Is this the same as the one you told me about last month?'

MODULE 3: Assessing
CARE

This module explores:
- how to strengthen the connection through the process of assessing
- the importance of attending and how to use it in practice
- how to develop a sensitivity to patients' cues
- how to use a holistic approach
- how to identify and apply different kinds of questions in order to gather further information and strengthen the connection.

In 'assessing' we aim to understand the patient's situation, perspective and feelings (and their attached meanings), and to place a patient's symptom and medical problems within the context of her life as a whole. This requires us to take a bio-psycho-social perspective. In making a holistic assessment, we need to listen to, and ask the patient directly, about how her symptoms or medical problems are influencing and being influenced by her life; about stress, emotions, and psychological issues; family, work, and other important life roles and relationships; and about how the illness is affecting her as an individual. For example, a recent life-threatening illness, such as a heart attack, may result in anxiety and stress, interfere with the patient's ability to work, raise concerns about intimacy and sexual activity, challenge her view of herself as strong and healthy, and raise existential or spiritual questions about life and death.

In assessing, we need to understand what the patient finds important in his life and how he makes sense of what is happening to him (McCormack & McCance, 2010). Core questions are, 'What are the issues and concerns from the *patient's* perspective?' and 'What does the patient want to achieve in relation to his health?' (Davis, 2006). Only by listening carefully and asking the right questions can we obtain insight into these issues.

Within the CARE Approach, there are four components of assessing:
1. attending
2. sensitivity to patients' cues
3. understanding the whole person
4. asking questions.

ATTENDING

To fully understand the patient and be able to respond meaningfully, we need to pay close attention to the content of the patient's story, the words that he uses to describe his experiences and how he makes sense of his story. This process is called 'attending'. Attending goes beyond listening, as we need to be fully present in the moment and wholly aware of what the person is communicating verbally and non-verbally. We need to resist reacting to what the patient is telling us and answering immediately to 'fix' his problem. We need to be aware of, but resist getting sidetracked by, our own thoughts, feelings and agenda as the patient's story unfolds. By listening carefully and accurately, we need to be able to 'hold' and 'stay with' the emotions that we feel.

The aim of assessing is to get to the heart of the matter – to understand how the patient sees her situation and obtain a picture of the patient's world, including her emotional state and the issues she is facing. We need to be sure that our own 'take' on the story does not distort the way we are listening and what we are hearing. Are we making judgements about the patient (based on partial evidence) or accepting her as she is and allowing her story to continue to unfold in its own way (Arnold & Boggs, 2007; McCabe & Timmins, 2006)? Listening in this way is not easy. It requires practice, reflection and experience before we can give our complete attention to our patients and for it to become a natural way of interacting. Through attending, we demonstrate that we are focused on the patient and communicate that we care about her well-being.

Exercise 3.1

View the clips then answer the following question.

Clip 1

Clip 2

In what ways do the healthcare practitioners in these clips show that they are attending/listening? (*See* 'Possible answers', p. 122.)

Attending is a powerful way to show that we respect and value the patient. However, if the patient feels that we are not paying close attention, do not give our time or are making assumptions or judgements about him, then he may feel that his concerns are being ignored or not taken seriously. In this situation, he may disconnect, become less open about his concerns and show signs of withdrawing from us. This is unlikely to be an empowering experience for the person.

Exercise 3.2

Twelve common behavioural barriers to listening are outlined following McKay *et al.*, 2009. In what ways and under what circumstances might these barriers interfere with your listening?

1. *Comparing*: Comparing interferes with listening because you are constantly assessing which of you, for example, knows best. While a patient is talking, you are thinking, 'If you think that is hard, let me tell you how hard it actually can be.'
2. *Mind reading*: Mind reading pushes you to look for hidden meanings rather than to listen to what is actually being said. You might not completely trust that the patient is being open or honest about what they really want, so you shift your focus to possible hidden meanings through changes in intonation or facial expression.
3. *Rehearsing*: 'Rehearsing' means trying to look interested while you are planning and practising (rehearsing) your response.
4. *Filtering*: You often listen to some things and not others to avoid problems. For example, if you are afraid of confrontations, you will pay attention to what mood the patient is in. If you perceive no 'angry' signs, you will stop listening.
5. *Judging*: Judging is often done so quickly that you do not realise that you have done it. However, when you subconsciously label someone as being unintelligent or lazy, you tend to pay less attention to what they are saying.
6. *Dreaming*: The patient's words trigger your own associations and you begin to daydream. When you resume listening, you find the patient is talking about something else, leaving you with a gap in their story.
7. *Identifying*: Whatever the other person says triggers memories of similar experiences you have had, then, before you know it, you either interrupt the other person's flow to tell your story or start to think about your own experiences. Meanwhile, you stop paying attention to the other person's story.
8. *Advising*: You are keen to fix the patient's problems and are ready with advice, reassurance and suggestions after only hearing a few sentences. You like to start your reply with, 'If I were you, I would . . .' However, while searching for advice, you sometimes miss what the real problem is.
9. *Sparring*: Regardless of what the other person is saying, you start to look for issues to disagree and argue with them about. A common example is making sarcastic comments to dismiss the patient's point of view (the so-called put-down).
10. *Being right*: You go to great lengths to try to prove that you are right, thereby using tactics such as making up excuses, talking over the other person in a loud voice or distorting the truth.
11. *Derailing*: As soon as you feel out of your comfort zone or bored, you change the topic of the conversation, make a joke or banter to prevent any further discomfort. Meanwhile, you stop paying attention to the other person's story.

(*continued over*)

12. *Placating*: You want to please and be nice regardless of the situation. You say things like, 'of course you are', 'absolutely', 'really' and find yourself unwittingly agreeing with everything the other person says.

Headings reproduced courtesy of New Harbinger Publications.

SENSITIVITY TO PATIENTS' CUES

In the course of a conversation, people might make throw-away comments or smile through gritted teeth when describing someone else, or sometimes a relative or carer will raise an eyebrow when a patient tells you that he can manage at home alone – these are all examples of cues. There are verbal and non-verbal elements that you may wish to pick up on and explore in the encounter. You might say something like, 'I get the impression that you don't find X an easy person to care for', for example.

Sometimes a patient will directly reveal a concern – for example, 'I am really worried' – but often such concerns are hidden and revealed only as cues. Cues range in degree of subtlety and can be easily missed or deliberately ignored. All cues are hints (conscious or unconscious) that there is more on the person's mind than she has articulated. It is probably best to assume that the patient is looking for a response from us. The extent to which patients feel able to discuss their emotions depends on many factors, such as the intensity of the feelings they are experiencing, how well they are coping, as well as their personality. However, as the healthcare professional, your own ability, willingness and sensitivity to detecting and exploring cues are crucial to the patient having the opportunity to express what she is feeling.

'Being open to patients' cues' can be described as carefully listening to the emotions behind the facts. From the patient's point of view, the way he feels is as important to him as the factual side of his medical condition. In one way or another during the encounter, the patient will show us how he is feeling and how much he is able to make sense of what is going on in his life.

Cues are opportunities to gain a better insight into what the patient is experiencing. By explicitly acknowledging them we can enhance our assessment and deepen our connection with the patient. If a cue is ignored or missed, especially when the patient has repeated it several times, the encounter is likely to be unsatisfactory for the patient and any subsequent responses and attempts to empower are likely to be unsuccessful.

Exercise 3.3

View the following clips that show a mixture of verbal and non-verbal cues made by patients, then answer the questions that follow.

Clip 1

Clip 2

Clip 3

1. What verbal and non-verbal cues do the patients give? What are the feelings that are revealed in the patients' voices or expressions? (*See* 'Possible answers', p. 122.)
2. Which cues do the practitioners pick up and which ones do they miss? (*See* 'Possible answers', p. 122.)
3. In what ways would you have dealt with the cues differently?

UNDERSTANDING THE WHOLE PERSON

'Understanding the whole person' means not characterising the patient only by her illness or one facet of her life. Taking other factors like gender, age, culture and life experiences into account in our interaction with patients is known as 'working holistically'.

To be able to understand the patient's experience of his illness, it may be important to learn about his work, family, home circumstances, support or personality (Brown *et al.*, 2001; Stewart *et al.*, 2003). The extent of this will of course depend on the context and nature of the encounter. However, it is often possible to take account of other aspects of a person's life whether you are taking a full history or seeing someone in a minor illness clinic; 'Who is at home with you?' is a question that might help here.

Understanding the whole person does not mean knowing her entire life story; rather, it means being able to understand where the patient is 'coming from' in the current encounter. Being able to put the patient's experiences of her illness in context is invariably helpful to both patient and practitioner.

If done in a non-intrusive and respectful manner, holistic assessment demonstrates that we are interested in the person with the illness. This helps in our assessment of the person and strengthens the connection with him (Platt & Gordon, 1999). Additionally, knowing about the relevant details of the patient's life will help us to give a more tailored response and increase our understanding of the patient's reactions to his health and illness (Stewart *et al.*, 2003).

Exercise 3.4

The following clips show different styles used by the same practitioner to obtain an understanding of the whole person. View the clips and observe how the healthcare practitioner demonstrates a holistic approach.

Clip 1

Clip 2

Clip 3

(*See* 'Possible answers', p. 122.)

ASKING QUESTIONS

Patients sometimes leave encounters with questions about what was said – 'I wonder why the nurse asked me that?' The questions that either you or the patient ask are an important aspect of the interaction, because they are a means of exploring and gathering relevant information. By being aware of different ways of asking questions we can gather information without coming across as being intrusive or superficial. If the patient considers questions intrusive, she may feel uncomfortable. However, too few or superficial questions may be interpreted as lack of interest. The number and type of questions depend to some extent on the patient's problems and how much information we need.

Certain questions used at appropriate times in an encounter can be particularly productive in yielding information.

1. *Open-ended questions* are general questions that encourage the patient to respond with more than one or two words. It is up to the patient how much information he gives. These questions often start with 'how', 'what', 'when' or 'can'. For example, 'What can I do for you today?' and 'From your point of view, what are the key things that are affecting your health?'

2. *Focused questions* define the area of enquiry more precisely but allow some scope in answering. For example, 'You said that you were feeling tense. What do you mean by that?'

3. *Closed questions* are those that can only be answered with specific responses, like 'yes' or 'no'. Continual closed questioning constrains the responses that the patient can give and prevents the patient from conveying her personal thoughts and feelings about her experiences. Often, they start with 'do', 'is' or 'are'. For example, 'Do you sleep well?', 'What is your name?' and 'How many children do you have?'

4. *Indirect questions* are rhetorical statements that imply a response is expected despite not grammatically being actual questions. These questions can be used as a way of gathering information without making the patient feel that he is being questioned

and they give the patient the chance to volunteer information. For example, 'In these situations some people find it difficult to get off to sleep.'

It is best to avoid the following two types of questions.

5. *Leading questions* imply specific answers, which are based on our assumption of what we think the patient should be experiencing. The most likely response is that the patient will agree passively with us. For example, 'You don't sleep well, do you?'

6. *Compound or double questions* mean that we ask more than one question at a time. The result is that we send a mixed message, and often the patient's answer is incomplete or confused. For example, 'Do you need to take sleeping pills to help you sleep, and do you still feel tired in the morning?'

Exercise 3.5

View the clip then answer the following question.

In what ways are the different aspects of assessing demonstrated in the clip? (The four aspects are: attending, sensitivity to patients' cues, understanding the whole person and asking questions.)

(*See* 'Possible answers', p. 123.)

A FINAL WORD ON ASSESSING

'Assessing' is the combination of gathering information regarding a patient's concerns, beliefs, views and expectations, *and* holding and sifting through that information to decide how best to respond and empower that individual. Thus, assessing in the CARE Approach is done on the basis of gathering the information that is unique to that individual and reflecting on this with the patient (or internally with yourself) as you begin to plan how best to respond. In many cases, as with connecting, this happens quickly and intuitively, without any need to reflect, think or plan. However, in many encounters, such intuitive and accurate responses may not be forthcoming. Such situations will thus require reflection and planning on the best ways forward in the next phase of the encounter or even after the encounter, in thinking ahead to future meetings with the same patient.

MODULE 4: Responding

CARE

This module explores:
- how responding interacts with connecting and assessing
- different ways to communicate our understanding of the patient's story
- why showing care and compassion is important
- why being honest and positive is important
- how to feel more confident in explaining things clearly and answering questions sensitively.

In the modules on connecting and assessing, we looked at ways of obtaining a picture of what the important issues are for the patient through attending, using a holistic approach and picking up on the patient's verbal and non-verbal cues. In addition, we saw that by building rapport and by paying close attention to what the patient tells us, we can enhance and deepen the therapeutic relationship.

Responding to the patient happens throughout the encounter. We do this verbally and non-verbally. In the process of 'responding', we follow-up and act on the findings of our assessment, from which we obtained an accurate picture of what the important issues are for the patient. In responding, we continue to pay attention to the patient's verbal and non-verbal cues to observe how she reacts to us. Being able to pitch our response to the patient's level of concern, emotion and understanding, as well as her state of mind, while addressing the issues that are important to her, will facilitate the patient's understanding and involvement in the encounter.

Within the CARE Approach, 'responding' means directly replying to the issues identified in assessing, as well as communicating and checking that we have accurately understood the patient's concerns before then acting on that understanding in a way that helps the patient. There are four aspects to responding:

1. demonstrating understanding
2. showing care and compassion
3. being positive
4. giving relevant information and clear explanations.

DEMONSTRATING UNDERSTANDING

When we listen to the patient, it is important to periodically check that we understand correctly the meaning of the story for the patient and do not inadvertently overlook or dismiss something that the patient regards as important. The task is to clarify various aspects of the story as sensitively as we can. If we can do this properly, we can communicate to the patient that we are taking his views and concerns seriously and that we respect him. By hearing us relate back to him what he has said, the patient may be able to see it in a slightly different light or it may help him articulate what he is trying to say. At times, this means that we will need to interrupt the patient's story. Helpful ways of demonstrating our listening and understanding are:

- *paraphrasing* or *summarising* the key points of the patient's story; for example, 'So, what you are saying is that you are confused about the different tablets and that you stopped taking them'
- *repeating key words and phrases* that the patient says; for example, 'so . . . you . . . have . . . no . . . energy?' or '. . . really tired . . .'
- *seeking clarification on* or *checking* statements that sound (slightly) confusing to us; for example, 'Can I just check with you that what you are saying is . . .?' or 'Am I right in picking up that you . . .?'

Through feeding back to the patient what is said and our understanding of this, we give the patient the opportunity to check and correct our understanding. Feeding back demonstrates that we are paying attention and communicates that we care. In making this explicit, the chances are that the patient will feel understood and appreciated, and we will create more opportunities to increase rapport and trust. In turn, this will strengthen the connection made at the start of the encounter and thereby encourage the patient to express herself more freely.

SHOWING CARE AND COMPASSION

Responding to the patient in a way that conveys our care and compassion is a key aspect of the CARE Approach. Showing care and compassion is a way to express our core values as healthcare professionals. Most of us went into and have remained in healthcare because we want to help people. Responding to our patients in caring and compassionate ways allows us to directly practise in the way that is consistent with our professional values. Responding gives voice to our values, beliefs and attitudes. When we feel compassion, we find it easier to listen deeply, understand more fully and demonstrate empathy. As a result, we are able to show concern that is both genuine and heartfelt.

One way of showing our involvement with the patient is through an empathic comment that reflects on his feelings. A reflection goes beyond the content of the patient's story (unlike paraphrasing or summarising), as it also takes into account the patient's non-verbal behaviour, the context of what he has said and the words used. For example, 'It sounds like your back pain is affecting really quite a lot of areas in your life. It is affecting your mood as well, because you are struggling to do all the activities that you were used to be able to do. Is that right, would you say?'

Another way of conveying that we are 'with' the patient at a human level is through validating the patient's reactions to her experiences as normal and understandable. A validation shows the patient that her reaction is appropriate and acceptable considering her experiences. For instance, in response to a patient who is crying and excusing herself, a practitioner might say, 'No, that is fine. It is very normal and understandable. It is a long time that you have been suffering the pain.'

Finally, empathic comments, like reflections or validations, demonstrate that we are attempting to understand the meaning behind the patient's words, value his perspective of the situation and support him.

Exercise 4.1

1. Think about how you would communicate to a patient that you care and can compassionately relate to her. (*See* 'Possible answers', p. 124.)
2. View the following clips. In what ways do the practitioners show care and compassion?

Clip 1

Clip 2

(*See* 'Possible answers', p. 124.)

BEING POSITIVE

Having a positive attitude requires us to be honest and, at times, frank, but never negative about the patient's problem. In all situations in healthcare, we should strive to offer hope and to empower. We need to be aware at all times that our approach and attitudes can have powerful effects on our patients, especially when they feel vulnerable and anxious.

We should not be insincere or dishonest, as the patient will quickly detect this. Remaining positive in our approach and attitude is perhaps the most important thing we can do to encourage our patients to see a clear way ahead of them. Indeed, research on the importance of different aspects of patient-centred care has shown that patients get better quicker when their doctors respond to their problems in a positive way (Little *et al.*, 2001).

Exercise 4.2

View the clips then answer the following question.

Clip 1

Clip 2

In what ways do the practitioners in the clips communicate that they are being positive? (*See* 'Possible answers', p. 124.)

GIVING RELEVANT INFORMATION AND CLEAR EXPLANATIONS

Two important aspects of responding to patients' concerns are giving factual information and explaining things. Explaining things clearly and in a way that is tailored to the patient, means that we give information and explanations in ways that take into account and are consistent with the patient's understanding, needs, values and beliefs. In addition, we observe the patient's reactions to check if we need to refine our explanations. When we communicate effectively and give clear information, we enable the patient to take more control and responsibility over her life.

Exercise 4.3

The following clips show two different ways of giving information to the patient. View the clips then answer the following questions for each clip.

Clip 1

Clip 2

1. In what ways are the practitioners' approaches to giving information and explanations different? (*See* 'Possible answers', p. 124.)
2. In what ways do the patients react differently in response to the practitioners' explanations? (*See* 'Possible answers', p. 124.)

The situation of giving information without taking into account the patient's understanding and needs is not uncommon within healthcare and indicates that, consciously or unconsciously, we are following our own agenda. For example, we might give him too much information, because it is an interesting topic to us or follow a set of tick boxes or script in our head that we feel we have to complete without being interrupted or taking into account what effect this has on the patient. In this case, our communication is less effective and can lead to misunderstanding and worry for the patient. Consequently, what we say may then be ignored or misinterpreted.

To match the amount and type of information to the patient's needs and preferences, we need to find out what and how much she wants to know. For example, is it the diagnosis, coping techniques or support available, the causes of the illness or side effects of treatment (or even just some aspects of these) that she is keen to learn more about? Asking and checking with the patient as we impart information is one way to match our information-giving to the patient's needs. For instance, 'I don't know how much you know about high blood pressure already?' or 'Can you say a little bit more about how you think it works?'

We need to be aware of terms that are so familiar to us that we assume patients share the same understanding. Words like 'migraine', 'virus' and 'depression' are part of everyday speech and most people are comfortable using them. This is also true of stories and explanations that we 'trot out' without thinking. While these accounts have become refined and honed over time spent interacting with patients, there is a danger that they may have lost their meaning. Medical words that are widely used will mean different things to different people and some meanings may be different from medical usage. It is often useful to check the patient's understanding of a particular technical term, because it is possible that he will hear the technical term again (Hull, 2005).

Exercise 4.4

Can you think of different reasons why you might use medical jargon?

(*See* 'Possible answers', p. 124.)

'Jargon' does not only refer to words found in the indices of textbooks, but to terms used by practitioners when communicating with one another. Being aware that we use certain jargon terms and appreciating why we do so will help us to become more aware of the way we interact with our patients.

Exercise 4.5

View the clip then answer the following question.

In what ways are the different aspects of responding demonstrated in the clip? (The four aspects are: demonstrating understanding, showing care and compassion, being positive, and giving relevant information and clear explanations.)

(*See* 'Possible answers', p. 124.)

A FINAL WORD ON RESPONDING

Responding builds on connecting and assessing, by requiring us to reply to the person's concerns. Responding involves both verbal and non-verbal aspects, as demonstrating understanding, showing care and compassion, being positive, and giving information and explanations are not just about what we say when we respond, but also how we say it.

Whether the way we are responding is effective depends on the context in which our approach is used. The patient's reaction to how we are responding is one way of gauging how we are being perceived. For example, the patient who smiles or visibly relaxes, and opens up a bit more following your response implies you have responded in an appropriate way. Keeping the focus on the patient, paying attention to cues and asking for feedback, if appropriate, will help us to keep our focus on the patient and maintain a person-centred approach.

MODULE 5: Empowering
CARE

This module explores:
- how empowering interacts with connecting, assessing and responding
- what 'appreciating the bigger picture' means
- how to help patients to take control and build their capabilities
- how to make a plan of action with the patient and confirm her or his understanding
- how to use empowering to build the patient's confidence.

'Empowering patients' is a concept that is difficult to define. It is sometimes described as sharing power with the patient or even surrendering power to the patient. It is a term that is widely used within the context of healthcare, and is widely regarded as having a positive impact on patient satisfaction and even some health outcomes.

Exercise 5.1

1. What does 'empowerment' mean to you? (*See* 'Possible answers', p. 126.)
2. In what ways can you empower patients? (*See* 'Possible answers', p. 126.)

Looking back at connecting, assessing and responding, you may already have noticed that empowering is a thread running throughout the CARE Approach. In the context of the CARE Approach, 'empowering' refers to helping patients to feel more in control of their health and healthcare. The focus of empowering in the CARE Approach relates to the following four aspects:

1. appreciating the bigger picture
2. helping patients to gain control
3. action-planning and confirming understanding
4. confidence-building.

APPRECIATING THE BIGGER PICTURE

We have already discussed the need for a 'whole-person' approach as part of assessing, but appreciating how a person's life and circumstances are affecting his health is so fundamental to empowering that we feel it is important to re-visit some of this again here.

In trying to empower, we need to have a good understanding of the context of the illness or condition against the backdrop of the patient's life. We need to know not only how the illness is affecting the patient's life, but also how life is affecting the illness. 'Appreciating the bigger picture' means using our knowledge and judgement sensitively to imagine how this person's condition might be influenced by her life circumstances. We can also indicate our understanding directly to the patient to check its accuracy.

For example, many of us will have an appreciation of the geographic areas that our patients come from – the housing type, the feelings of safety within the community, the public transport links and the access to supermarkets and other services. The patient's address, recorded in his case notes, may give an indication of certain aspects of the patient's life. However, the danger here is that we may make assumptions and pigeonhole people. Knowing that a patient with chronic obstructive pulmonary disease lives in a high-rise building, for instance, might tell us nothing more than that there are restrictions on his social life when the lifts break down (which they might do on a frequent basis). Knowledge of the local area may help us to understand why some patients are late for appointments, for example, or why our advice about healthy living never seems to be taken up. Although we can make a real difference to the way that patients feel within the encounter, the effect might not endure after the interaction when patients return to their daily lives. Trying to understand people's lives helps us to appreciate why our best efforts might not always have the effect we hope for and why people sometimes struggle to make sense of the advice we give.

It might be useful to use open questions such as, 'What is life like for you?' and 'Who is at home with you?' and to respond to statements like, 'It's difficult, you know' with 'Tell me about that . . .'

It is helpful to find out about what restricts patients in their daily lives, as people might feel disempowered in their domestic lives or workplaces. Patients may talk about flights of stairs, an unsympathetic boss or a challenging family member. The patient may have an informal role as a carer, which may mean that she does not have much time for her own health, and awareness of this might lead to the patient being able to access entitlements and other assistance. Connecting with people in terms of this bigger picture and trying to appreciate and understand the complexities of their lives can not only enhance our relationship with patients but also help in goal-setting and tailoring treatment, and in helping patients to make realistic and appropriate decisions about care.

Patients will respond very differently to a healthcare practitioner who is trying to understand them and their lives than to a practitioner who gives advice and instructions that do not fit with the challenges of daily living. As healthcare professionals, we need to appreciate how the patient feels about pushing himself to take control and what failure might mean for him – for example, confirmation in his own mind of repeated failure, or ridicule by friends, family and others.

HELPING PATIENTS TO GAIN CONTROL

As healthcare professionals, we often give patients information about their condition and how to manage it, advise them of available support services and provide them with health-promotion literature.

In some cases, we teach patients how to undertake tasks such as checking their peak flow and administering injections. Giving information and teaching skills of self-management can be empowering. However, some of this information is complex and some of these skills are quite technical, so it is seldom sufficient to give the patient the information and to show her the skills without supporting her and reinforcing the instruction.

It can be useful to identify a patient's strengths and his prior accomplishments. In addition, it can be helpful to explore with the patient what he feels he can do to improve his situation.

Taking control of your condition can be frightening, particularly if you fear being left to get on with it on your own. However, helping patients to take control is about encouraging them to take responsibility for more self-care rather than all care. It may be better to think of it as gaining more control rather than taking absolute control.

This usually involves exploring with the patient what she can do to improve her health or situation. Therefore, our role becomes that of coach and mentor – nurturing, involving, demonstrating and positively reinforcing. By being involved as active partners in their care, patients are encouraged to take more control and responsibility, based on their strengths and capabilities.

Some treatment options may require an adjustment in lifestyle, behaviour and associated coping skills to meet certain health goals. Information about treatment options may be hard to take on board, so may require a simple structured pace. The patient needs to feel comfortable to be able to discuss health goals or treatment options, and we need to be sensitive to how he is responding as we give information and check understanding.

Fundamental to shared decision-making of any kind is that the patient understands her situation up to the point that she feels able to make choices she is comfortable with. Making their own choices will help patients gain a sense of control and independence. Access to information and support from others with the same condition, for example, self-help groups, can be useful for some patients.

'Gaining control' means having the self-belief that you can achieve something as much as it means being able to be successful in mastering certain skills or finding the motivation to change something in your life.

Exercise 5.2

1. What does 'self-management' mean to you?
2. Listen to the audio recording in which a healthcare professional talks about self-management. How do your answers to exercise 5.2 question 1 relate to the practitioner's view? You can read the transcript of the recording on self-management in Appendix 5 (p. 69).

ACTION-PLANNING AND CONFIRMING UNDERSTANDING

'Making a plan of action with the patient' relates to defining options on how to proceed. Options can involve agreeing on health goals and making choices about treatment options. We should resist making assumptions about how much the patient wants to be involved in his care, and we need to find out how much and in what ways he wants to engage in his care. To be effective, a shared plan of action needs to be realistic in terms of what is achievable.

The patient cannot really exercise choice unless we facilitate a shared understanding of the problem or illness, which needs to be defined in a clear manner on which both agree. Employing a holistic approach by focusing on the patient's feelings, needs, experiences and lifestyle will help to make the problem concrete and relevant.

An 'action plan' sets out the management of a condition and within this plan there may be specific goals. It is helpful to make a distinction between long- and short-term goals. A long-term goal for a young person with asthma might be for her to play a whole game of football without having to come off the field because of shortness of breath. A short-term goal might be to control wheeze on minimal exertion through optimal inhaler use over the next few weeks. The time frame defines whether a goal is short or long term, but so does the likelihood of the goal being achievable, and this has to be negotiated. Achieving goals, whether short or long term, is about helping people become much more confident in their ability to cope with and manage their illness.

Exercise 5.3

Watch the clips then answer the question that follows.

The clips show different approaches to exploring with patients what they can do to improve their situation, identifying choices that are realistic for them and seeking their preferences actively.

Clip 1

Clip 2

In what ways do the practitioners differ in their approaches? (*See* 'Possible answers', p. 126.)

In Clip 2 of Exercise 5.3, the physiotherapist and the patient talk about goal-setting. In the audio recording, the physiotherapist explains in more depth what she means by 'goal-setting' (a transcript of this recording can be found in Appendix 5, p. 69).

An important aspect of making a plan of action with the patient is to check frequently that the patient understands the information you give and that he is clear about what course of action you have both decided on. Having a clear understanding enhances the patient's ownership of his health and enables him to manage his situation better (Hull, 2005).

To check whether our communication has been effective, we can ask the patient to feed back to us what has been agreed on during the encounter. For example, we can say, 'I want to be sure that I explained X properly, because it can be confusing. Can you tell me what we agreed?' or 'Just so that I am clear, what are the kind of things we agreed on? Just to make sure we both know.' Another way is to give the patient ample opportunity to ask questions or to clarify things. For example, by asking, 'Does that sound alright to you?', 'Is this what you expected from your visit today?' or 'Is there something else that you would like to talk about or ask me?'

CONFIDENCE-BUILDING

People are more likely to attempt something when they believe they can do it and if they think they have the ability to do it. 'Self-esteem' and 'self-efficacy' are two concepts that can help us to make sense of 'confidence-building'. 'Self-esteem' is the belief someone has regarding her own worth or value, and her respect for herself, while 'self-efficacy' is described as a person's beliefs in her capabilities and competences in order to cope with and feel in control of her life (Bandura, 1995).

Recognising and nurturing the strengths and competences of the patient is an important part of helping him to gain a sense of control over his care and health.

Empowering, in the sense of fostering the patient's beliefs in his own capabilities and competences (Ashcroft, 1987), can take many different forms.

We can confidence-build through follow-up encounters of an appropriate frequency. At these regular encounters, we can empower patients by endorsing, confirming, praising, affirming and congratulating them. We may also need to help them to refine techniques and to offer instruction. Patients want us to be honest and to show appropriate levels of support and follow-up. We can reduce a patient's feelings of vulnerability and increase her sense of security by using strategies such as saying, 'If you don't feel you are better, come back in tomorrow morning.'

Exercise 5.4

View the clips then answer the question that follows.

Clip 1

Clip 2

Clip 3

In what ways do the healthcare practitioners foster the patients' beliefs in their own capabilities and competences? (*See* 'Possible answers', p. 126.)

As insightful practitioners, we will appreciate our patient's successes no matter how large or small, acknowledge these successes and use them as milestones in a patient's journey. Gaining confidence brings hope and a determination that goals can be achieved and that successful plans or pathways can be made to achieve goals.

Exercise 5.5

View the clip then answer the question that follows.

In what ways are the different aspects of empowering demonstrated in the clip? (The four aspects are: appreciating the bigger picture, helping patients to gain control, action-planning and confirming understanding, and confidence-building.) (*See* 'Possible answers', p. 126.)

A FINAL WORD ON EMPOWERING

Throughout the descriptions of each component of the CARE Approach, it has been made clear that each cannot be seen as an isolated part. This module on empowering has been no exception.

The potential empowering outcomes of the CARE Approach are highlighted throughout the book. These are that patients feel understood, valued and respected; involved in their care in a way they feel comfortable with; able to self-manage; and that the interaction supports their overall well-being. The next section of the book puts all four components together and shows them in action.

OVERVIEW OF THE CARE APPROACH

Connecting	Assessing
1. Establishing rapport	1. Attending
2. Accepting the patient as a person	2. Sensitivity to patients' cues
3. Effective non-verbal communication	3. Understanding the whole person
4. Allowing the patient to tell his or her 'story'	4. Asking questions
Responding	**Empowering**
1. Demonstrating understanding	1. Appreciating the bigger picture
2. Showing care and compassion	2. Helping patients to gain control
3. Being positive	3. Action-planning and confirming understanding
4. Giving relevant information and clear explanations	4. Confidence-building

MODULE 6: Putting it all together

This module explores:
- how the CARE Approach components interact and work together
- the CARE Approach as a two-way process
- the spirit of the CARE Approach
- ways of supporting yourself in the CARE Approach.

THE INTEGRATION OF THE CARE APPROACH COMPONENTS

Although we have presented the CARE Approach components as individual aspects in the previous modules (2–5), you will have probably realised by now that the four domains of the CARE Approach do not necessarily follow this simple linear order of connecting → assessing → responding → empowering. Indeed, in everyday practice, most encounters will have a varying combination of the four components occurring, in a varying order.

Exercise 6.1

View the clips then answer the questions that follow.

Clip 1

Clip 2

Clip 3

1. Write down what components of the CARE Approach you think are happening at which time over the course of each encounter. You can use the blank graph to map this out by placing a cross against the component you think is occurring as each interaction moves along the time scale.

(*See* 'Possible answers', p. 127.)

(*continued over*)

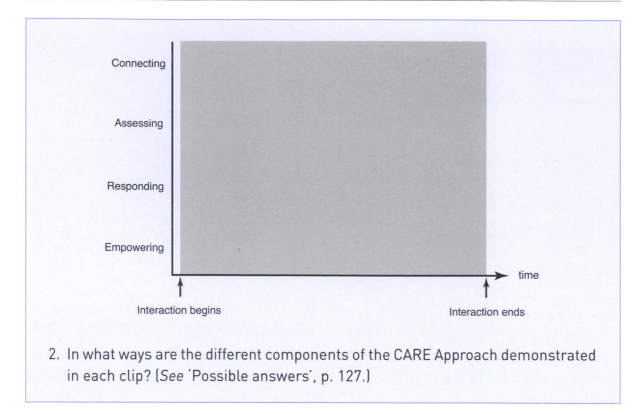

2. In what ways are the different components of the CARE Approach demonstrated in each clip? (*See* 'Possible answers', p. 127.)

Clearly there are many ways in which the CARE Approach components can come into play in an encounter. Some encounters may be mainly about connecting with some assessing, and the response may simply be to set a date for the next consultation. Some encounters may have repeated cycles of differing combinations of C-A-R-E, or indeed experienced practitioners may be combining the different components at the same time. Figure 1 illustrates how a skilled practitioner might combine and move between the domains of CARE during an encounter.

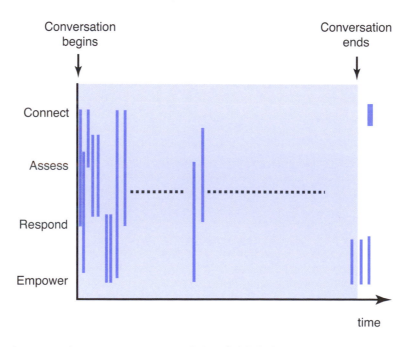

FIGURE 1 Mapping out the components of the CARE Approach in a typical encounter

In this hypothetical encounter (Figure 1), at the start of the consultation, the practitioner both connects and assesses at the same time (e.g. by making the patient feel at ease with a polite and warm introduction and assessing the patient's non-verbal behaviour). If the patient were to seem anxious or ill at ease, the practitioner could then rapidly respond to this by offering a smile, or slightly changing her or his head or body position. This may then help the patient relax a little, and the practitioner could continue connecting, letting the patient tell her story, and assessing again by listening and looking for non-verbal and verbal cues, and responding to these as they arise. Thus, during the course of an encounter, there are an infinite number of possible ways to enact the CARE Approach. If we are highly skilled communicators, and are fully engaged in the encounter, such responses occur naturally, based on our insight and awareness. Under such conditions, the encounter is almost like an impromptu piece of jazz music performed by expert musicians.

THE CARE APPROACH AS A TWO-WAY PROCESS

What is no doubt also obvious to you by now is that the CARE Approach is not something that you 'do' to the patient; rather, it is a two-way process that is all about your interaction with the patient. If you are with a patient that you get on with very easily, it is likely that you both connected at first glance (maybe when you went to call the patient in the waiting room and made eye contact), perhaps because you already know each other well from previous encounters or you have instantly 'clicked', as discussed in Module 2, 'Connecting'.

The connecting–assessing–responding–empowering (in whatever order and combination they occur) may well then simply run automatically, without any effort on your part. Such encounters are of course a joy (unless they involve breaking bad news or suchlike) and make the job of being a healthcare professional seem very easy and satisfying.

However, as we all know, not all encounters follow such an easy, smooth course. This may be because, in most consultations, especially if we do not know the patient well, there is an element of 'feeling our way' in the encounter. What is very likely, though, is that the patient is also going through a similar process and making an active effort to connect with us, assess us (verbally and non-verbally), and respond to us in active ways. The patient may even go to great lengths to try to empower us in our difficult work.

Exercise 6.2

View the clips then answer the question that follows.
In what ways can the CARE Approach be applied to the way the patient is interacting with the healthcare professional?

Clip 1

Clip 2

Clip 3

(*See* 'Possible answers', p. 128.)

We may meet a patient who we feel a dislike for (and may not even know why) or who, despite all our best efforts, may be clearly not responding to what we are saying or suggesting. In such circumstances, it may be tempting to struggle on with the consultation regardless, and bring it to a speedy close. However, a better way might be to slow down, take a deep breath and take a moment to notice what is actually going on. Notice how you are feeling in your mind and body. You may be feeling tense, irritated, angry or frustrated. You might notice a slight tightness in your throat or abdomen, or that your heart is racing. Just noticing how you are feeling may be enough to allow you to slightly relax, to acknowledge and let go of these feelings, or to simply let them be there without acting on them. You may be surprised to find that this may be enough to also help the patient feel less tense, as you begin to tune in to what she is actually feeling and the possible reasons for this. It is never too late in a conversation that has somehow got off on the wrong foot to turn things around (or to at least try to do so). Perhaps you need to ask the patient how she is feeling about what you have been saying, or to offer a simple apology if you have clearly misunderstood something. If you are sincerely motivated to help the patient, most difficulties and misunderstandings can be worked through at an early stage, to the mutual satisfaction of both patient and practitioner.

Exercise 6.3

In what ways does the practitioner address the situation in the clip?

(*See* 'Possible answers', p. 129.)

THE SPIRIT OF THE CARE APPROACH

So far, we have discussed the individual components of the CARE Approach, how these can interact in a cyclical, non-linear way, and how the encounter with the patient is an active interaction involving the practitioner and the patient, rather than simply the health professional carrying out a detached, objective clinical procedure.

This then brings us to what actually lies at the core of the CARE Approach, to what comprises its 'essence' or 'spirit'. In our view, the heart of the CARE Approach is a combination of empathy and awareness: awareness of ourselves, awareness of the patient and awareness of the interaction between us, moment by moment.

Such awareness, and our capacity for this, determines the authenticity, depth and presence inherent in our interactions with patients.

WAYS OF NURTURING AND SUPPORTING YOURSELF AND OTHERS IN THE CARE APPROACH

This section looks at some ways to successfully nurture and develop awareness in the context of the blend of skills, techniques and attitudes that we have covered so far in this book in describing the CARE Approach.

The first point to make is to look after yourself. Healthcare can be a stressful and demanding profession. It is important that you maintain a healthy work–life balance and promote self-care for yourself just as you do for your patients. If you are feeling stressed or burnt out, or are suffering from other problems that are affecting your well-being, then it is unlikely that you will be performing at work to your full potential. At worst, your own poor well-being may be actively limiting your ability to deliver high-quality care to your patients. If you have significant concerns in this area, you need to discuss this with your line manager, occupational health service or GP.

Looking after your own health means paying attention to the things that affect your health and that only you can do something about – that is, lifestyle factors such as ensuring you exercise, have a healthy diet, drink alcohol within safe limits, stop smoking and so on. Looking after your body also has major benefits for your mind – exercise, for example, is an excellent treatment for stress or mild depression. Other ways of looking after your well-being include spending time with loved ones and close friends, doing hobbies you enjoy and having regular breaks or holidays.

For some people, religious or spiritual beliefs and practices are an important way of developing awareness and fostering well-being. The cultivation of 'mindfulness', for instance, has a long history in Eastern spiritual traditions such as Buddhism. However, mindfulness can be taught as a set of skills independent of any religious belief system. A popular form of accessible, secular mindfulness training is the mindfulness-based stress reduction (MBSR) educational programme devised by Jon Kabat-Zinn (Kabat-Zinn, 2004). This is run over eight sessions and involves training in mindfulness meditation, integrated with teaching on psychological understanding and models of stress.

There is increasing empirical evidence of the benefit of MBSR to healthcare professionals (Irving *et al.*, 2009) and may therefore be helpful in developing the interpersonal and self-awareness that are core to the CARE Approach. This includes developing reflective self-awareness and strategies to manage the emotional and physical impact of work, maintaining personal well-being and managing stress.

MODULE 7: The CARE Approach with colleagues and in teams

This module explores:
- the importance of teamwork
- barriers to effective team working
- successful team working
- connecting, assessing, responding and empowering in the context of teamwork.

Thus far we have concentrated on the relationship between the healthcare professional and the patient. We now broaden our focus to consider working with other people, across professional boundaries and in multidisciplinary teams.

In 2011, NHS Education Scotland commissioned a study to evaluate the CARE Approach. Teams in five healthcare settings participated in the study and completed the CARE Approach book through peer facilitation (Heywood *et al.*, 2012). An interesting outcome of the study was that the majority of the participants noticed an improvement in communication not just with patients but also with staff, and this influence on working relationships and the sharing of information was regarded as positively affecting patients' experience of care. One of the peer facilitators reported afterwards:

> I think we've had conversations that I've never had. I've been qualified 25 years and done tons of postgraduate qualifications and training, and delivered and facilitated quite a lot of training. And I would say it's been quite a revelation to me to hear what colleagues think and how they really feel (Heywood *et al.*, 2012).

Therefore, this module focuses on the importance of team learning and how the CARE Approach may enhance interactions with colleagues as well as with patients.

As the number of person-to-person interactions increases, so does the number of opportunities both for success and for things to go wrong. The following suggested exercises and examples are derived from the components of the CARE Approach and aim to facilitate learning and reflection on some of the relational aspects of working with others and on our own perceptions of our place in this. This module is written for all members of all teams, irrespective of the team structure or hierarchy, and, as with previous modules, it can be used by individuals, groups and organisations.

TEAMWORK

All professional regulatory bodies emphasise working in teams, and indeed the General Medical Council (GMC) of the United Kingdom makes explicit the value of teamwork in terms of purpose and value, effectiveness and efficiency, and the chain of responsibility.

A 'team' can be defined as a group of people working together for a common purpose, whose members cooperate and support one another. A key characteristic of a team is that its tasks are interdependent, so that the members have to communicate, coordinate actions and cooperate to accomplish each one (Salas *et al.*, 2008).

During our professional lives, we must collaborate with other people in teams that are usually tightly, although sometimes more loosely, defined. For some, teamwork is easy because the members all share the same goals and interests. Sometimes people do not perceive themselves as part of any team, perhaps because this has not been made apparent through work, task or purpose.

Exercise 7.1

1. What is your response to the terms 'team' and 'team working'? What thoughts come to mind? What feelings do you associate with these terms?
2. Which teams, if any, do you consider yourself a member of at work?
3. Take one team that you belong to. What words would you use to describe this team?

Teams take many different forms. There are several common assumptions made about teams and it is worth reflecting on these for the teams of which you are a member. It is often assumed that team members have common aims and goals, each member has a distinct and important role, most teams have leaders and teams are able to measure their performance. These assumptions are not always true. Further, many assume that a team's structure is static, and this is also not necessarily true.

We have probably all experienced being a member of teams that function well and teams that function badly. Although the type or structure of teams that we find ourselves in varies, there tend to be some fundamental features common to all good experiences. These include clear communication, the handling of conflict, clearly defined roles, commitment to decisions, specific goals, accountability, paying attention to results, agreed levels of autonomy and a culture of respect in which differences and openness are valued and everyone's voice is heard.

Ample research (e.g. Borrill *et al.*, 2001; Powell *et al.*, 2012; Xyrichis & Lowton, 2008) shows that, in practice, building effective teamwork is complex and difficult to sustain. There are many barriers to effective team working, such as a sometimes literal and damaging culture of blame, and the use of exclusive language and jargon. Many teams are multi-professional or multidisciplinary and there may be clear differences in levels of accountability and independence. In addition, there can be differences in perceptions of ethical issues such as confidentiality. There can be differences in accountability because of employer or funding stream, and there can be differences in rights to the use of certain facilities. Preconceptions about the training and status of other professionals can also be a barrier to effective team working. People in uni-professional teams do not necessarily have it any easier. Barriers to effective teamwork in uni-professional teams include poor communication, absence of affirmation, poorly articulated or shared vision, and condoning 'bad' behaviour.

CONNECTING, ASSESSING, RESPONDING AND EMPOWERING IN TEAMS

Connecting is about working together as *people* and recognising and acknowledging differences without making judgements or putting others down. It is about recognising the training of others and their contribution to the team – recognising that colleagues tell their story through the work that they do.

Thus, connecting will help to develop and maintain trust, which is a precondition to openness within a team. Without trust, it can be daunting to part with information that may expose our lack of knowledge or shortcomings, especially when we cannot predict what response we will receive from others. Levels of trust between people are not static and tend to fluctuate and change over time.

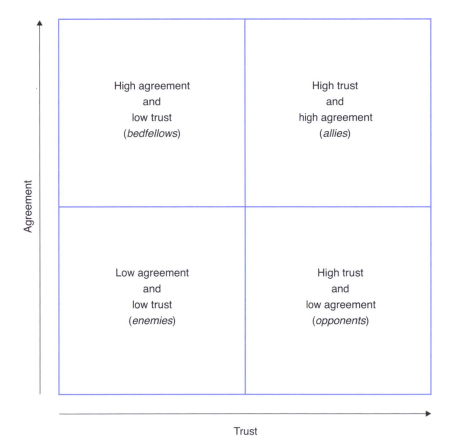

FIGURE 2 Trust agreement matrix. Reproduced with the kind permission of Peter Block from Block P. *The Empowered Manager: positive political skills at work.* San Francisco, CA: Jossey-Bass; 1987.

Block (1987) developed a matrix that highlights the link between trusting someone and agreeing with that person in a working relationship (*see* Figure 2). Block offers a label for each of the four broad groups and these are included in the figure. We may agree to a greater or lesser extent on an issue (e.g. the way resources are used), but our level of trust about the way we pursue the issue is established through relationship and experience. By using these two dimensions of trust and agreement, we can develop an insight into our working relationships.

Exercise 7.2

1. Think about the different ways you react to people in your team when they agree or disagree with you about an issue. Think about those who you trust highly and then those who, for a host of reasons, you do not trust greatly. When your team has to make important decisions, how important are levels of trust and agreement in achieving goals? For example, as a team leader, it can be a formative experience to have your ideas challenged by someone with whom you have a high level of trust. Similarly, if you are pushing for agreement in a climate of low trust, how sustainable are the changes or ideas you are promoting?
2. Think about a high-trust team or culture you have worked within. What helped to create that culture?
3. From your experience, in what ways can trust be broken and rebuilt within teams?
4. What is the level of trust like in your current team?

Assessing is about attending to colleagues and being sensitive to their context and role. It is about asking appropriate questions about their role. Key to assessing is being able to listen in such a way that the other person feels heard and understood. This can be hard to do in the busy workplace in which we multitask and always seem to be catching up with ourselves. Research (e.g. Borrill *et al.*, 2001; Brown *et al.*, 2011) has shown that misunderstanding about roles and confusion over the vision of a team leads to friction and poorly developed relationships between team members.

It may be useful to consider where the organisational focus is and, indeed, where the power lies in your team. In fact, consider what benefits all parties derive from being a part of the team. Within a team, some members may be 'employers' while others are 'employees' and this can create a particular dynamic.

Consider the validated multi-source feedback (also known as '360-degree feedback') instruments used by many organisations and endorsed by medical royal colleges as part of appraisal and personal development. The domains within these feedback instruments demonstrate the importance that medical royal colleges place on valuing colleagues and the complementarity of their roles. If you are not familiar with these instruments, take a look at www.equiniti360clinical.com/. These instruments measure how our colleagues – clinical and non-clinical – perceive us, by responding to a series of questions and statements. Many organisational-development departments within health-service organisations will have licenses for different 360 tools that they can administer for a team.

One way of gaining insight into our relationships with others – in this case, at work – is by using the 'Johari window' (Luft, 1984). Figure 3 is a standard representation of the Johari window in which each quadrant (or pane) is the same size.

The Johari window can be used to guide personal development and team development and as a means of better understanding relationships. Thus 'self' can mean you, the individual, or the group in question. Likewise, 'others' can mean other individuals or other groups. Each quadrant is an area of knowledge the relative proportions of which can change depending on the situation or context. So, as a person becomes embedded in a team and grows in confidence, the size of their 'open area' (quadrant 1) enlarges, ultimately reducing other quadrants particularly the 'unknown area' self (quadrant 4). The open quadrant is the knowledge that is shared about values, attitudes and skills and contributes most to effective communication between an individual and others and in teams. The more people know about each other, the less our interactions are affected by mistrust or misunderstanding.

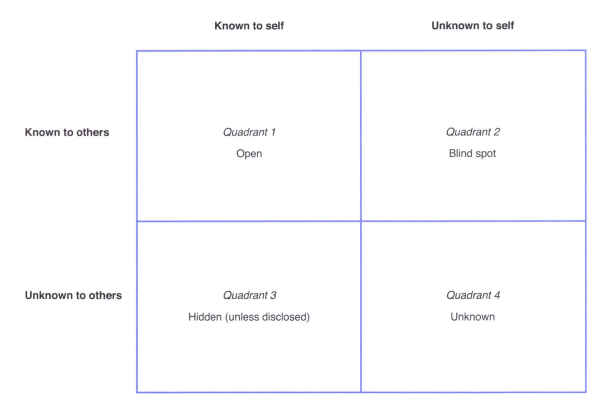

FIGURE 3 Johari window

Exercise 7.3

For this exercise, work with a colleague and take turns answering the questions.
1. Quadrant 1: Identify one or more things in relation to your role that your colleagues already know (e.g. your patient caseload is very heavy, there is nowhere private to sit and have a coffee break).
2. Quadrant 3: Identify one or more things in relation to your role that your colleagues are not likely to know (e.g. you don't like your uniform, the time taken to travel to and from work, an aspect of your set of personal values that informs your practice, an aspect that you enjoy about your chosen profession).
3. Quadrant 2: Invite a colleague to say something about his/her perception of your role. This may be unknown to you. If a 'blind spot' is identified, how does this feel?
4. Reflect on how identifying such knowledge can affect the relative size of each of the quadrants.

Connecting and assessing are underpinned by communication that acknowledges each team member and makes them feel valued. *Responding* is about seeking clarification and demonstrating understanding, which will also help to make people feel heard and understood, and make it less likely that barriers will be built. Connecting and assessing will help us to modify our response to the circumstances and interaction that we encounter. Returning to the domains within multi-source feedback instruments, giving clear explanations in ways that other team members understand is clearly of huge importance within teams.

Exercise 7.4

Think for a while about making change in the workplace – for example, reorganising rotas or the office. How would that change affect a typical day for the people involved? Are there potential areas where conflicts or misunderstandings might arise?

Colleagues can often react emotionally to change while those who have planned the changes offer rational reasons to explain why the new way is better. Unless we connect and assess, we will not hear the emotion and acknowledge it. We have to raise our own awareness of others and their roles in the workplace.

The most common reasons for conflict in teams include professional and personal identity, physical space, and control over workload such as situations where individual workloads, and systems and processes are not fair. There can be differences and disagreements around principles such as the patient as part of the team, or the contribution of complementary medicine to patient care and well-being.

Other common problems in teams include differences in goals, differences in line management of people in the same team and variations in support within teams. Another frequent issue is where there are perceived problems with communication. Further, the ways in which conflict is managed, difficult questions are asked and significant events are dealt with may cause difficulties for people in teams. The ways in which teaching and learning are offered for teams, and the different ways teaching and learning are valued and rewarded by different professional groups may cause conflict too.

People deal with conflict in different ways, depending on what is at stake, the circumstances and those involved. Collaboration is often seen as the preferred way of dealing with conflict, because it involves an exchange of views and ideas that takes into account the perspectives of all involved. For example, the use of language such as 'Yes, and how about . . .' rather than: 'Yes, but how about . . .'. Other phrases that may help in collaboration are: 'What is it about X that is important to you?' and 'How would you approach X? . . . My view is . . .' Demonstrating understanding of the other person's viewpoint and giving relevant information and clear explanations about one's own viewpoint will increase the chances of successful collaboration.

Although collaboration is seen as a positive approach to working, there are other forms of conflict resolution that may be more appropriate in different circumstances. Two examples are 'accommodating', which means reaching consensus by agreeing with the other person, but often at the expense of your own needs or point of view, and 'compromising', which refers to looking for the middle ground (Thomas & Kilmann, 2007).

Although we may not be able to *empower* others directly, we can try to create the conditions that are likely to help a person feel empowered. Delegation without explanation, building confidence or checking that everyone understands roles and responsibilities will not help team members feel empowered.

The literature on followership reminds us that people within teams and organisations need to feel significance; a sense of community; and challenge, excitement and edge (Goffee & Jones, 2006). We have to ensure that team members feel valued and ensure that we affirm their contribution to the outputs and purposes of the team, and be genuinely interested in their development and skill set.

Based on a review of studies on empowerment, Spreitzer (1996, 2008) identified four common positive beliefs held by people who feel empowered at work – meaning, competence, self-determination and impact.

1. *Meaning*: how much the purpose of the job fits with our beliefs and values, and contributes to the overall goals of the organisation.
2. *Competence*: having confidence in our ability to do the work.
3. *Self-determination*: feeling trusted and having a degree of choice and freedom in deciding how to do the work.
4. *Impact*: having the ability to influence the outcomes at work and the work environment.

Taken together, these beliefs help create an understanding of how our work fits into in the bigger picture of healthcare delivery.

Exercise 7.5

Reflect on each of the four dimensions of the CARE Approach in terms of your workplace. Use the following chart. If you feel comfortable doing so, discuss your reflections with a colleague.

CARE Approach dimension	What it means to me in the workplace	What I already do to achieve this	What else I could do to achieve this
Connecting	(E.g. others showing a genuine interest in me as a person)	(E.g. make eye contact)	(E.g. let others tell their story/point of view and try to avoid interrupting)
Assessing	(E.g. feeling heard and understood)	(E.g. pay attention to cues)	(E.g. pay attention to my barriers to listening)
Responding	(E.g. modifying responses to the circumstances that I encounter)	(E.g. check I have understood people correctly)	(E.g. consider that others may be right)
Empowering	(E.g. feeling trusted)	(E.g. I thank or acknowledge others)	(E.g. thank people and praise them when due)

A FINAL WORD ON TEAM WORKING

'Team building' is an evolutionary process that starts with an awareness of our own ways of interacting with colleagues, and a willingness to listen and to understand the contributions of others. The CARE Approach provides a shared language when discussing issues of team working. It places a very high value on communication. Each person in a team has information that someone else in that team needs in order to achieve effective and successful healthcare outcomes.

The CARE Approach is not a rigid set of rules and is not linear in time. We tend to connect and reconnect with colleagues during the course of a day and return to assessing and responding at various times. The CARE Approach raises awareness of communication issues in teams and of those elements of working relationships that contribute to positive and effective teams.

MODULE 8: Facilitating the CARE Approach

This module explores:
- different styles of facilitation
- activities for group work
- preparation for, and the tasks of, facilitation
- setting up one or more CARE Approach sessions.

Teams, small groups and practices may wish to work together on the CARE Approach. You may find it easier if you appoint someone to facilitate your group learning. What you, as a group, do will depend on the duration and frequency of your meetings, and the size of your group.

There are different ways in which people perceive the roles of facilitators; in this case, as the facilitator, you will be more of a nurturer and less of a subject-matter expert or educator (a 'guide on the side rather than a sage on the stage'!).

There is often little time in which to achieve learning and you will want to engage with people in your group quite quickly. There are several ways in which you can help people to relax into the dynamic of the group. Many people use an icebreaker exercise, but this depends on how well members know each other and how much time is available. Similarly, how much time you put into establishing group rules may depend on how much time you have to work on this current project. Remember: if you do write group rules, make sure that you don't labour this process.

You will need to vary your style according to the task and the group's stage of development. You should expect to move in and out of different facilitation styles.

The styles can be described as:
- directive: like a teacher; *'Please do this . . .'*
- cooperative: working with the group; *'Let's explore . . .'*
- autonomous: letting the group drive itself; *'Okay, I'll leave you to get on with this'.*

ACTIVITIES FOR GROUP WORK

There are various different activities you can use for group work. Use these activities wisely and don't try to use all of them in one session. If you think that the group's energy level is dropping, take a break and check how they are getting on. Alternatively, you can try a different activity that alters the dynamic – for instance, you could ask your colleagues to chat – or 'buzz' (*see* 'Buzzing' following) – with their neighbour about an issue.

The following activities are most useful.

Brainstorming

In brainstorming, usually you would invite contributions from group members and record these on a flip chart or board. There are very few rules to this method, but while you are writing the contributions on the flip chart or board:

- do not yourself challenge or allow other participants to challenge a contribution (if it is an 'odd' contribution, write it in one corner of the flip chart/board and offer to come back to it later, possibly even after the meeting)
- write down contributions word for word.

Buzzing

This is when you ask two or three people to discuss an issue for a few minutes before reporting back to the group.

Snowballing

People are asked to pair up to discuss an issue, then each pair joins with another to form a group of four. After a further period of discussion, the group of four joins with another group of four into a group of eight. After a last round of discussion, each group of eight reports back. Post-it notes can be used to generate ideas.

There are very few rules with this method. However, specifically, do not throw any Post-its away during the process.

Jig-sawing

You can use this technique to discuss several domains or aspects of a much larger concept. Group members should form into small groups and take one aspect of a situation, discuss this and then report back to the whole group.

When directing discussion, it is a good idea to give each small group a task such as, *'Come up with three things that might . . .'*

Role playing

This is probably the most risky of all techniques because of performance anxiety, the fear of exposure, and the risk of embarrassment to colleagues who have not engaged in this before.

PREPARATION AND THE TASKS OF A FACILITATOR

As a facilitator, you have group tasks and process to take care of. 'Process' is about planning the session, keeping to time and agenda, watching the dynamic and taking care of all members of the group. Your 'tasks' are about ensuring that the group achieves what is agreed and required in the session.

Your tasks include:

- gaining the involvement of all members of the group
- dealing with conflict and difficulties
- achieving an understanding of various views
- being unbiased
- clarifying group decisions
- incorporating individual inputs
- planning the sessions
- being clear about who is coming, why they are coming and for how long
- making sure you have a comfortable space
- taking care of refreshments
- timetabling each session
- telling the group members what to expect – timeline, outcomes and so on.

SETTING UP ONE OR MORE CARE APPROACH SESSIONS

The CARE Approach can be delivered flexibly, although the most obvious way is to present it as four related sessions – one for each domain. Map out what you are going to do. Ideally, you will want the opportunity to meet over a number of sessions and for 2 hours each time.

Set learning outcomes for each meeting and establish a programme with timings. You are likely to be meeting a group of people who recognise themselves as members of the same team, so you may not opt for an icebreaker activity. You should make clear the outcomes for the session and aim to achieve these.

Take 5–10 minutes to establish a number of 'group rules', such as confidentiality, mutual respect, not talking over each other, the minimisation of interruptions (e.g. agree to switch off mobile phones) and a commitment to attendance. One simple approach is to write one or two points on a flip chart and invite group members to come up with others.

The group-rules exercise is about creating a place of trust and mutual understanding, so you may find that you need to explicate what members understand by terms such as 'confidentiality' – for example that nothing discussed in the group is taken outside the group.

Each module of this CARE Approach book starts with a bullet list of what the module explores. This list of learning outcomes should be used to describe what you (as a group) are going to find out about in each particular session. The focus is on obtaining an understanding of the component(s), relating the component(s) to experiences of the group and how to go about applying the CARE Approach in the work setting.

For the second and subsequent meetings of the group, ensure that you factor in time at the start of a session to 'check-in' and specifically to see if there is any unfinished business from the last time. You might want to ask the group members what they remember from last time or what they have done with the learning from the last session. Group members will have processed the material from the previous meeting in different ways and taking time at the start can yield rich reflections. It is also a great way to re-iterate key learning from last time.

Outline what you are going to do during the session. It may be a good idea to give a brief account or definition of what the particular CARE domain you will look at in the session is about; for example: *'Connecting is what happens when you "click" with someone. What do you think we mean by this, and what does it mean for us as healthcare professionals?'*

Then let group members know how you are going to run the session:

'Over the next hour we will . . .'

'We will spend the first 30 minutes doing X and then we will go on and cover Y and we will finish on time at 2 p.m.'

Plan the timings for a session. It should be possible to follow the pattern of the module in a 2-hour session.

Familiarise yourself with this pattern, which is the same in each module:

- introduction to the domain (10 minutes)
- the domain (20–30 minutes)
- exercises: (1 hour)
  - ❯ clips
  - ❯ tasks.
- summary (10 minutes).

Photocopy the exercises you wish the group members to undertake, as some colleagues will prefer to annotate a spare sheet rather than to use their book. Always make sure that you signpost where you are by making sure that group members see the page that you are on and make sure they are all on that page before you continue. Given the tasks you have to complete in the available time, it will be helpful for all in the group if you mark the progress from one domain to another.

Start each new domain by asking group members what they think it means and then work through the domain using the exercises and clips.

Useful strategies as a facilitator

There are some useful strategies that you can employ as a facilitator.

- Use 'time out' and 'time in': Take 'time out' of the discussion by suspending the dynamic and then return to it ('time in'). This can be used if group members are getting nowhere in their discussions and you think some clarification is needed.

You can also use this to ask members how they are doing – *'Let's take time out – how are you getting on?'* Other examples of what you can say when the group seems to be getting stuck include:

❭ *'That's a good question, hold on to it and we'll come back to it'*
❭ *'We have a lot to get through, can we move on?'*
❭ *'That's interesting – what do the rest of the group think?'*
❭ *'We seem to be getting bogged down here – is this helpful, useful?'*
❭ *'Is this an issue that affects you all?'*

- Useful statements: It is helpful to have phrases you can use when things get tough; for instance: *'Thank you for that. Do other people feel we are getting stuck in our discussions?'* and *'Does anyone have a different view?'*
- 'Parking' things: If colleagues raise issues that don't fit in or are rather unexpected, state that you think it best to set the issue to one side for the present. Write down the issue in one corner of your flip chart/board and draw a box around it. Commit to speaking to the individual afterwards or to dealing with it at the beginning of the next session.
- Checking: Periodically check that the group is keeping up with the process and tasks.

Challenges

From time to time you will have to deal with challenging groups and individuals. Broadly, possible challenges include:

- someone who talks incessantly
- someone who doesn't talk at all
- someone who disrupts the group, tries to undermine you and other contributors
- someone who uses humour to derail the process
- the group having difficulty reaching a decision
- the withdrawal of one or more members
- members becoming aggressive
- low energy within the group
- the emergence of personal issues.

There are many different and sometimes quite specific ways to deal with group challenges. In some cases, you may even have to suspend the session for a while, but always try to seek consensus and agreement before moving on. Try to get the group to examine the process: *'What is going on here – can anyone help?'* (Review some of the already-mentioned useful phrases!)

Another, potentially risky, strategy is 'checking' by inviting feedback on the process on a regular basis. Be prepared to adapt if the group agrees changes to the format.

Dealing with questions can be a challenge. Remember to avoid the trap of being pulled into a one-on-one with the questioner when responding. A useful step-by-step process is to:

1. take the question

2. repeat it back to the group
3. give answer to the whole group.

Getting it right

There is a lot to manage in running a session. The following list may help you.

- If you are going to use technology, make sure that it works.
- Practise the session in advance.
- Try to have the following available, even if you don't think you will need them:
  - ❭ flip chart, whiteboard, and the correct pens
  - ❭ Blu-tack
  - ❭ Post-it notes
  - ❭ handouts.
- Be clear, concise and compelling.

The items in the checklist that follows are typical of the areas on which you might give feedback to a colleague who has taken on the role of facilitator; it is useful to consider these elements as you prepare to facilitate a session yourself:

clarity and content of presentation
appropriate use of resources
verbal and non-verbal communication
teaching aids
background knowledge of the subject
introduction, aims and objectives, and learning outcomes
structure
explanation, clarification, questioning, reinforcement, feedback, describing, encouraging analysis
your verbal and non-verbal communication as a teacher
dealing with different learning needs
appropriateness of pace and timing
variety of activities of interaction used.

Giving feedback to group members can be tricky. Try to be sensitive and consider the following:

- raise awareness of issues
- be descriptive rather than judgemental – don't use 'good' or 'bad'; use 'I', as in, 'I felt that . . .'
- describe behaviour rather than the individual or aspects of their personality
- share information and check understanding
- avoid overloading.

FURTHER READING

There are many resources on facilitation. If you would like to find out more, the following are two examples you might want to look at.

By the NHS:
- NHS Institute for Innovation and Improvement. *Facilitation Guides*. Coventry: NHS Institute for Innovation and Improvement. Available at: www.institute. nhs.uk/quality_and_service_improvement_tools/quality_and_service_ improvement_tools/facilitation_guides.html (accessed 8 November 2013).

On role playing:
- Mind Tools. *Role Playing: preparing for difficult conversations and situations*. London: Mind Tools. Available at: www.mindtools.com/CommSkll/RolePlaying. htm (accessed 8 November 2013).

A FINAL WORD ON THE CARE APPROACH

We hope that you have found the CARE Approach stimulating and useful in your work as a healthcare professional. To develop a more empathic, person-centred way of interacting takes practice, and is both challenging and exciting. A journey of a thousand miles starts with a single step, so any small changes you make to your interactions with patients based on the CARE Approach may lead to surprisingly large benefits for them.

Remember that the CARE Approach is not a one-way street, and that the people we call 'patients' are generally also trying their best to interact with us in a fruitful way. In healthcare encounters, a win–win situation – in terms of productive and effective human interactions – is what everyone is striving for.

It may seem daunting in a busy healthcare setting, and you may at times feel overwhelmed. You are a professional doing an important job, and you want to do it to the best of your abilities. However, you do need to stay within your professional boundaries, and if you feel that you are out of your comfort zone, you need to seek the support of your team and your line manager. As discussed in this module, you also need to look after your own well-being, both in and outside the workplace.

Thank you very much for taking the time to study and reflect on the CARE Approach. We wish you continuing success in your important work.

APPENDICES AND ADDITIONAL INFORMATION

APPENDIX 1: The CARE Measure

© Mercer, 2004

Please rate the following statements about today's consultation *Please tick one box for each statement and* <u>answer every statement</u>	Poor	Fair	Good	Very good	Excellent	Does not apply
How was the doctor at . . .						
Making you feel at ease *Being friendly and warm towards you, treating you with respect; not cold or abrupt*	❑	❑	❑	❑	❑	❑
Letting you tell your 'story' *Giving you time to fully describe your illness in your own words; not interrupting or diverting you*	❑	❑	❑	❑	❑	❑
Really listening *Paying close attention to what you were saying; not looking at the notes or computer as you were talking*	❑	❑	❑	❑	❑	❑
Being interested in you as a whole person *Asking/knowing relevant details about your life, your situation; not treating you as 'just a number'*	❑	❑	❑	❑	❑	❑
Fully understanding your concerns *Communicating that he/she had accurately understood your concerns; not overlooking or dismissing anything*	❑	❑	❑	❑	❑	❑
Showing care and compassion *Seeming genuinely concerned, connecting with you on a human level; not being indifferent or 'detached'*	❑	❑	❑	❑	❑	❑

(continued over)

Please rate the following statements about today's consultation *Please tick one box for each statement and* answer every statement						
Being positive Having a positive approach and a positive attitude; being honest but not negative about your problems	❏	❏	❏	❏	❏	❏
Explaining things clearly Fully answering your questions, explaining clearly, giving adequate information; not being vague	❏	❏	❏	❏	❏	❏
Helping you to take control Exploring with you what you can do to improve your health yourself; encouraging rather than 'lecturing' you	❏	❏	❏	❏	❏	❏
Making a plan of action with you Discussing the options, involving you in decisions as much as you want to be involved, not ignoring your views	❏	❏	❏	❏	❏	❏

DESCRIPTION

The Consultation and Relational Empathy (CARE) Measure is a consultation process measure that has been developed by Prof Stewart Mercer and colleagues in the general practice departments of Glasgow University and Edinburgh University in Scotland. It is based on a broad definition of 'empathy' in the context of a therapeutic relationship within the consultation. The wording reflects a desire to produce a holistic, patient-centred measure that is meaningful to patients irrespective of their social class, and has been developed and applied in over 3000 general practice consultations in areas of high and low deprivation in the west of Scotland.

The scoring system for each item is 'Poor' = 1, 'Fair' = 2, 'Good' = 3, 'Very good' = 4, and 'Excellent' = 5. All 10 items are then added, giving a maximum possible score of 50, and a minimum of 10. Up to two 'Does not apply' responses or missing values are allowable, and are replaced with the average score for the remaining items. Questionnaires with more than two missing values or 'Does not apply' responses should be removed from the analysis.

The theoretical background and validation of the CARE Measure can be found in:

- Mercer SW, McConnachie A, Maxwell M, *et al.* Relevance and practical use of the Consultation and Relational Empathy (CARE) Measure in general practice. *Fam Pract.* 2005; **22**(3): 328–34.
- Mercer SW, Maxwell M, Heaney DH, *et al.* The Consultation and Relational Empathy (CARE) Measure: development and preliminary validation of an empathy-based consultation process measure. *Fam Pract.* 2004; **21**(6): 699–705.

- Mercer SW, Reynolds WJ. Empathy and quality of care. *Br J Gen Pract*. 2002, **52** Suppl.: S9–S12.

The CARE Measure can be used free of charge. The intellectual property rights rest with the Scottish Executive. The measure may not be used on a commercial basis without the consent of the lead author and the Chief Scientist Office of the Scottish Executive Health Department, on behalf of the Scottish Ministers. If you would like more information, please contact:

Prof Stewart Mercer
Academic Unit of General Practice and Primary Care
Institute of Health and Wellbeing
College of Medical, Veterinary and Life Sciences
University of Glasgow
1 Horselethill Road
Glasgow G12 9LX
United Kingdom
stewart.mercer@glasgow.ac.uk

For further information, and to download the measure please visit:
www.caremeasure.org

APPENDIX 2: Person-centredness

'Person-centredness' is becoming a popular term. In healthcare literature and policy documents, the term is often used interchangeably with 'patient centred', 'client centred' or 'relationship centred'. Although there is no consensus on the definition of person-centredness, in general it is used to describe healthcare delivery that has at its core consideration for the patient in terms of their human experience and with respect for their values. The focus is on the process of interaction, and it is recognised that this process is influenced by the qualities and attitude of the health practitioner (McCormack & McCance, 2010; Mead & Bower, 2000).

In recent policy documents, such as the *'Gaun Yersel!': the self management strategy for long term conditions in Scotland* (Long Term Conditions Alliance Scotland, 2008), the focus is on the needs of *people* and not *patients*. Although we support this word usage throughout the CARE Approach, we use 'person-centred' when referring to the overall approach but the term 'patient' (instead of 'person', 'client' or 'service user') when it seems appropriate in the context of individual encounters.

APPENDIX 3: Background to film scenarios

Note: When the filming of the simulated encounters between the actor-patients and practitioners took place, only the actor-patients knew the scenarios. The practitioners were largely unaware of the kind of issues the actor-patients would address during the interaction.

ROBERT FARLANE

Mr Farlane is a 49-year-old plumber seeking treatment for chronic right-knee pain. He lives with his wife and two teenage children. His wife does not work and his 14-year-old son was born with cerebral palsy. Mr Farlane is worried about the impact that this pain will have on his work and ability to support his family and care for his disabled son. In this encounter, he talks with the physiotherapist.

MRS MCDONALD

Mrs McDonald is a 65-year-old woman who has noticed that her big toenail is discoloured. She is retired and lives with her husband in a first-floor tenement flat. She has a history of type 2 diabetes (for 20 years or so). Based on the stories she has heard from other people, she is worried that her toenail could lead to other more serious things like losing her leg. She discusses her issues with the podiatrist.

RHONA LESLIE

Rhona is 38 and unmarried. She lives with her mother and works as a cashier in an accounts company. She is a nervous person and recently this has been getting worse. She now has episodes of 'palpitations', where her heart seems to beat very rapidly. Last week was the first time she had passed out during an episode of anxiety and this made her frightened. She has come to the GP for advice.

MRS BOYLE

Mrs Boyle is a 47-year-old woman seeking treatment from the physiotherapist for chronic low-back pain. The pain started many years ago for no apparent reason and has gradually worsened to its current level. As a result, she has been off work and put on weight. She lives with her husband who has a demanding job. At times, she feels she is not contributing to the home and she limits her social activities due to the fear that the pain will be aggravated. She is worried that something is seriously wrong but that nothing can be done to help.

BILLY ANDERSON

Billy is dependent on a variety of drugs that he obtains regularly from various GPs and other sources. He does not consider himself an addict, as he just needs these things to help him sleep and to control pain. Poor sleep has been a constant problem for him. He used to be a surveyor. He is divorced with two children who he is not in contact with. In the encounter, he aims to persuade the doctor to issue drugs (temazepam).

MRS DALRYMPLE (1)

Mrs Dalrymple is an older woman who has multiple conditions. On the death of her sister Rosie, she began helping to look after her sister's grandchildren as well as her own. She lives with her husband who has recently been made redundant. Due to her circumstances, she has not paid much attention to her health. She is worried about her feet. She has a good relationship with the GP who knows her relatively well through previous visits in the clinic.

MRS DALRYMPLE (2)

Another visit by Mrs Dalrymple to the GP.

MRS JEANIE HALL (INITIAL VISIT)

Mrs Hall has been a widow for about a year. She finds life difficult. She suffers from multiple conditions (including diabetes and heart problems). She no longer works and is becoming more and more socially isolated. The GP has asked her to come to the practice to discuss her circumstances. Mrs Hall is not sure what to expect at the visit.

MRS JEANIE HALL (FOLLOW-UP VISIT)

Mrs Hall returns to the clinic for her second visit to discuss with the GP how she has got on after her initial visit during which they had agreed a plan of action. She is more at ease this time, as she knows what to expect of the interaction. She feels that she has made progress and openly discusses her reunion with her daughter and a long-lost friend.

APPENDIX 4: Background to the CARE Approach

The background to the CARE Approach relates to two developments. In May 2010, The Scottish Government published *The Healthcare Quality Strategy for NHSScotland*. The strategy focuses on person-centredness and on communicating in an empathic manner. A core priority is to deliver 'caring and compassionate staff and services' (p. 1). The drive towards care that focuses on the patient's needs and the relationship between the practitioner and the patient is collaborative and holistic, and not isolated to Scotland, as it is consistent with policy developments at international level.

Moreover, in *The Healthcare Quality Strategy for NHSScotland*, the CARE Measure (*see* Appendix 1, p. 61) is recommended for use across the whole of the NHS in Scotland as one of the ways to obtain patient feedback regarding the provision of person-centred care. The CARE Measure was developed and validated by Professor Mercer and colleagues in the universities of Glasgow and Edinburgh almost 10 years ago and is now widely used in Scotland, the UK more broadly and internationally. This patient-rated experience measure assesses the quality of healthcare interaction in terms of the 'human' aspects of the encounter from the patient's perspective. The measure can be used to give direct feedback to practitioners on their strengths and weaknesses in terms of empathy as experienced by the patients (Mercer *et al.*, 2004). The CARE Measure is also being used in GP appraisals, and in the assessment of GPs in training across the UK as part of the new Membership of the Royal College of General Practitioners (MRCGP) workplace-based assessment. Although initially developed and validated in general practice, the measure has also been validated in secondary care settings and is currently being used in nursing and allied health professions (AHPs) as well as in medical specialities. A major formal validation of the measure in nursing and AHPs in Scotland is being carried out by Stirling University, Scotland, and is near completion.

The CARE Approach book is designed to translate the key aspects of this vision of person-centred, empathic encounters at policy level into a resource for practice. Additionally, the CARE Approach supports the use of the CARE Measure. The CARE Approach can be used in conjunction with the CARE Measure, but the approach can also be used as a stand-alone tool.

DEVELOPMENT

The CARE Approach was developed at the University of Glasgow, Scotland. The starting point of the development of the CARE Approach were the 10 items of the CARE

Measure. The book makes the link between the 10 items of the measure and the four aspects of the approach. Through researching a wide scope of health and communication literature, drawing on shared experience of teaching communication skills at undergraduate and postgraduate levels in multidisciplinary settings, discussing this approach with healthcare practitioners and through meetings with The Scottish Government, the book is in its first edition.

WHAT THE CARE APPROACH IS NOT

The CARE Approach is *not*:

- a method purely about clinical assessments. It goes beyond this by addressing the human (including the emotional) aspects that are part of the encounter
- a tick-box exercise that promotes a right/wrong way approach to care
- a rigid model. Instead it is a general framework that recognises that each encounter is unique, dependent on the context and requires a flexible approach
- a linear model that maps exactly onto the beginning, middle and ending stages of an encounter. The four components are an integrated cyclical process and each component can occur at any moment during the interaction.

APPENDIX 5: Transcripts of audio recordings from exercises

EXERCISE 5.2: SELF-MANAGEMENT

Self-management is really trying to get the patient to take some responsibility for managing their symptoms, especially with chronic conditions, where some people are looking for something external to fix them and sometimes that is just not possible. So, self-management is trying to encourage and empower the patient to find different tools and techniques, which work for them on a day-to-day basis, which will help them to manage their symptoms and their life better, so that they have a better and improved quality of life, while possibly having some help from external support, but that is not the long-term answer. They have to find within themselves the different tools and techniques which work for them on a day-to-day basis, which will help improve their life.

EXERCISE 5.3: GOAL-SETTING

In relation to the clip, we mention medium- to long-term goal-setting with the patient, specifying work as a goal. So that is something that we would sit down and we would agree. We would look at the short-term goals again liaising with the SMART acronym and ensuring that everything was Specific, Measurable, Achievable, Realistic and Timely. Work on the short-term goals initially, so that she can see that she is actually achieving something, which will boost the confidence, self-esteem and motivation to continue with following the goals. Potentially, after an assessment, if the work was not an immediately achievable goal, then discussing with the patient and hopefully agreeing that that potentially would be a medium- to longer-term goal. But focusing on the small, achievable ones initially to give them that inner strength and confidence and self-esteem.

APPENDIX 6: Additional bibliography

In addition to the references referred to in the text, the following materials also influenced the development of the CARE Approach book.

BOOKS AND ARTICLES

- Alexander MF, Fawcett JN, Runciman PJ, editors. *Nursing Practice: hospital and home; the adult*, 3rd ed. Edinburgh: Churchill Livingstone; 2006.
- Brooker C, Waugh A. *Foundations of Nursing Practice: fundamentals of holistic care*. London: Elsevier; 2007.
- Bunt L, Harris M. *The Human Factor: how transforming healthcare to involve the public can save money and save lives*. London: NESTA; 2009. Available at: www.nesta.org.uk/sites/default/files/the-human-factor.pdf (accessed 6 December 2013).
- Caproni PJ. *Management Skills for Everyday Life: the practical coach*. 3rd ed. Upper Saddle River, NJ: Pearson Education; 2012.
- Chant S, Jenkinson T, Randle J, *et al.* Communication skills training in healthcare: a review of the literature. *Nurse Educ Today*. 2002; **22**(3): 189–202.
- Coetzee SK, Klopper HC. Compassion fatigue within nursing practice: a concept analysis. *Nurs Health Sci*. 2010; **12**(2): 235–43.
- Crane R. *Mindfulness-Based Cognitive Therapy: distinctive features*. Hove and New York, NY: Routledge; 2009.
- Docherty C, McCallum J, editors. *Foundation Clinical Nursing Skills*. Oxford: Oxford University Press; 2009.
- Firth-Cozens J, Cornwell J. *The Point of Care: enabling compassionate care in acute hospital settings*. London: The King's Fund; 2009. Available at: www.kingsfund.org.uk/sites/files/kf/field/field_publication_file/poc-enabling-compassionate-care-hospital-settings-apr09.pdf (accessed 27 October 2013).
- Goodrich J, Cornwell J. *Seeing the Person in the Patient: the Point of Care review paper*. London: The King's Fund; 2008. Available at: www.kingsfund.org.uk/sites/files/kf/Seeing-the-person-in-the-patient-The-Point-of-Care-review-paper-Goodrich-Cornwell-Kings-Fund-December-2008_0.pdf (accessed 27 October 2013).
- Hartley P. *Interpersonal Communication*. 2nd ed. London: Routledge; 1999.
- Howie JG, Heaney DJ, Maxwell M, *et al.* Quality at general practice consultations: cross sectional survey. *BMJ*. 1999; **319**(7212): 738–43.
- Hutchinson TA, Dobkin PL. Mindful medical practice: just another fad? *Can Fam Physician*. 2009; **55**(8): 778–9.

- Krasner MS, Epstein RM, Beckman H, *et al.* Association of an educational program in mindful communication with burnout, empathy, and attitudes among primary care physicians. *JAMA.* 2009; **302**(12): 1284–93.
- Lloyd M, Bor R. *Communication Skills for Medicine.* 2nd ed. London: Harcourt; 2004.
- McCabe C. Nurse-patient communication: an exploration of patients' experiences. *J Clin Nurs.* 2004; **13**(1): 41–9.
- Morse JM, Bottorff J, Anderson G, *et al.* Beyond empathy: expanding expressions of caring. *J Adv Nurs.* 2006; **53**(1): 75–90.
- Neuman M, Bensing J, Mercer S, *et al.* Analysing the 'nature' and 'specific effectiveness' of clinical empathy: a theoretical overview and contribution towards a theory-based research agenda. *Patient Educ Couns.* 2009; **74**(3): 339–46.
- Perkins DD, Zimmerman MA. Empowerment theory, research, and application. *Am J Community Psychol.* 1995; **23**(5): 569–79.
- Perry B. Conveying compassion through attention to the essential ordinary. *Nurs Older People.* 2009; **21**(6): 14–22.
- Rungapadiachy DM. *Self Awareness in Health Care: engaging in helping relationships.* Basingstoke: Palgrave MacMillan; 2008.
- Sanders P. *First Steps in Counselling: a students' companion for basic introductory courses.* 3rd ed. Ross-on-Wye: PCCS; 2002.
- Sanders P, Frankland A, Wilkins P. *Next Steps in Counselling Practice: a students' companion for degrees, HE diplomas and vocational courses.* 2nd ed. Ross-on-Wye: PCCS; 2009.
- Schreiner K. *Medical Assisting Made Incredibly Easy: therapeutic communications.* Baltimore, MD, and Philadelphia, PA: Lippincott Williams & Wilkins; 2009.
- Silverman J, Kurtz S, Draper J. *Skills for Communicating with Patients.* 3rd ed. London: Radcliffe Publishing; 2013.
- Skelton J. *Language and Clinical Communication: this bright Babylon.* Oxford: Radcliffe Publishing; 2008.
- Stewart M. Towards a global definition of patient centred care. *BMJ.* 2001; **322**(7284): 444–5.
- Stilgoe J, Farook F. *The Talking Cure: why conversation is the future of healthcare.* London: Demos; 2008. Available at: www.demos.co.uk/files/Talking%20 cure%20final- web.pdf?1240939425 (accessed 27 October 2013).
- Sully P, Dallas J. *Essential Communication Skills for Nursing.* London: Mosby; 2005.
- Thomas KB. General practice consultations: is there any point in being positive? *Br Med J (Clin Res Ed).* 1987; **294**(6581): 1200–2.
- van der Cingel M. Compassion and professional care: exploring the domain. *Nurs Philos.* 2009; **10**(2): 124–36.
- Van Nuland M, Thijs G, Van Royen P, *et al.* Vocational trainees' views and

experiences regarding the learning and teaching of communication skills in general practice. *Patient Educ Couns.* 2010; **78**(1): 65–71.

● Walsh M, editor. *Watson's Clinical Nursing and Related Sciences.* 6th ed. Edinburgh: Bailliere Tindall; 2002.

● Watzlawick P, Beavin Bavelas J, Jackson DD. Some tentative axioms of communication. In: *Pragmatics of Human Communication: a study of interactional patterns, pathologies and paradoxes.* New York, NY: WW Norton; 1967. pp. 48–71

● Wright KB, Sparks L, O'Hair HD. *Health Communication in the 21st Century.* Malden, MA, Oxford and Melbourne: Blackwell; 2008.

Frequently asked questions

Is it possible to use the CARE Approach when you feel under time pressure?

Yes. The CARE Approach can be applied in situations in which we feel under pressure. It is a guide on how to put person-centredness into practice regardless of workload. The focus is on our 'attitude' and communication and how these can be incorporated into our lives and routinely used in practice without creating more work. Research conducted within primary care indicates that a practitioner's empathic attitude (as perceived by patients) leads to higher enablement, regardless of consultation length (Mercer *et al.*, 2012).

Is it difficult to learn the CARE Approach?

Developing skilful communication habits takes practice. Often we have developed a way of interacting with patients on 'automatic pilot' without questioning whether that is the best way. The CARE Approach book is a supportive tool to review and reflect on the impact of your own communication skills. It is not about changing your personality, but about adapting your approach and responses in healthcare encounters to communicate in a person-centred manner. Therefore, as long as you are willing to be open to a way of approaching people that may or may not be familiar to you and to (gradually) become aware of how you can put the approach into practice, you will be on the right track. Sometimes the CARE Approach may seem too difficult (or even far-fetched) to put into practice, and in these cases we tend to go back to the ways we are used to in dealing with patients. This is a natural process. Learning to deal with patients in a person-centred way needs commitment and can be a continuous process.

Does this book not just describe what we are already doing in practice?

You may already be working in a way that is 'person centred', and in this case the book will just remind you of what you are doing. However, if you are not, you may identify new insights and discover a different way of working that builds the tasks around the patient, rather than the other way around.

What about the patient side of the encounters?

It is important that communication in healthcare be a two-way process. Just as we are assessing and responding, so is the patient. That is why communication can be such a challenge! The CARE Approach provides a tool for you to feel better equipped to interact with your patients. It cannot predict the patients' reactions to the way you interact or the content of what you say. However, the book describes how to pay attention to patients' emotional cues and level of understanding and highlights the importance of checking with patients what you are picking up from them.

Will the CARE Approach help me with patients who seem to want me to tell them exactly what to do?

Patients sometimes ask, 'What do you think I should do?' and say things like 'You just tell me and I'll do it'. The CARE Approach can help us to think about how we respond to these questions and statements. Creating time to explore why a patient feels like this can be fruitful. It will also be consistent with the CARE Approach that we use with patients at other times. At times, we may need to give direct instructions to patients, and the ways in which we share these and agree on them are key elements of the CARE Approach.

Further reading

The following books are only a handful from the many useful books on the subject of communication, empathy and person-centredness that are available.

- Davis CM. Patient *Practitioner Interaction: an experiential manual for developing the art of health care.* 4th ed. Thorofare, NJ: SLACK; 2006.

  This is a very accessible book on self-awareness, human behaviour and skills for communicating effectively with patients. At the end of each chapter is a series of exercises.

- McCabe C, Timmins F. *Communication Skills for Nursing Practice.* London: Palgrave McMillan; 2006.

  This is a good introductory book to communication from a patient-centred and therapeutic perspective. It includes information on different models of communication as well as exercises.

- McCormack B, McCance T. *Person-Centred Nursing: theory and practice.* Oxford: Wiley-Blackwell; 2010.

  This book brings together a variety of resources on person-centredness and caring. It offers a practical approach to developing ways of caring in a person-centred manner.

- McKay M, Davis M, Fanning P. *Messages: the communication skills book.* 3rd ed. Oakland, CA: New Harbinger; 2009.

  This book extensively covers different types of communication and includes exercises. Its techniques can be applied personally as well as professionally.

- Silverman J, Kurtz S, Draper J. *Skills for Communicating with Patients.* 3rd ed. London: Radcliffe Publishing; 2013.

  This book provides the reader with a comprehensive set of communication skills.

- Stewart M, Brown JB, Weston WW, *et al. Patient-Centered Medicine: transforming the clinical method.* 3rd ed. London: Radcliffe Publishing; 2014.

  This is a practical book introducing the patient-centred model of medicine. It is illustrated with real case examples. It has a section focusing on research on patient-centred care.

THE **CARE** APPROACH WORKSHEET

MODULE 1: What you bring to the encounter

EXERCISE 1.1

1. What is your response to the word 'caring'? What thoughts come to mind? What feelings do you associate with the word?

2. What are the aspects of your job that make it possible for you to practise in ways that you consider to be caring?

EXERCISE 1.2

1. What features best characterise you when interacting with a patient? For example, do you tend to reassure, listen well or take control?

2. Consider the types of patient interactions you have. List situations when you are you most likely to be patient oriented and when are you most likely to be task or disease oriented?

   Patient oriented

   Task or disease oriented

3. For each of the situations you have listed in 2, describe whether you are aiming to meet your own needs or the patient's needs.

EXERCISE 1.3

1. Think of yourself as a patient. What would the ideal doctor or nurse be like and how would they behave towards you?

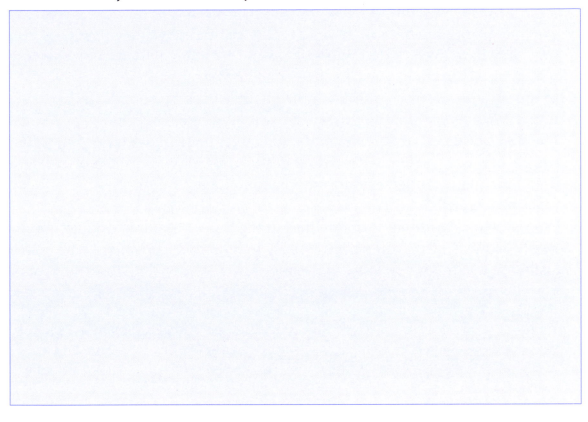

2. In what ways are these behaviours important?

EXERCISE 1.4

This is called the 'respected figures' exercise.

1. In the first column, write down at least two and up to five people who you deeply respect for the way they have led or lead their lives. You do not have to respect everything about them, but in one or more significant ways, you should admire how they have lived or do live. These people could be living or dead, famous or not famous, known to you personally or simply heard about.

2. In the second column, write down the qualities each person had or has that you respect. What was it about them that you admired? Then look for individual qualities or clusters of qualities that stand out. A particular quality may stand out simply because you know inside that it is of great importance to you, or because the same quality appears next to more than one person on the chart – possibly described in a slightly different way.

3. Write down up to three such qualities in the third column. If you are not being overly idealistic, these qualities are likely to represent *root* values, which are crucially important for you to try to live by.

Who do you deeply respect for the way they have led/lead their life?	What are the qualities this person had/has that you particularly respect?	What are the three key qualities this person had/has that you particularly respect?
1.		
2.		
3.		
4.		
5.		

From Hawkins (2013).

EXERCISE 1.5

Make a list of your top three root values, and consider the following questions.

Consider the values you have identified in Exercise 1.4, the respected figures task. Do you live these values yourself? In what ways do you try to live these values in your personal and professional life? What are the things that help you bring these values into your everyday life? What are the things that prevent this from happening?

Can you make any changes in your work or personal life that would allow you to live your values more fully?

MODULE 2: Connecting

EXERCISE 2.1

View the clips showing different approaches then answer the following question.

In what ways do the healthcare practitioners create a good first impression with the patients?

EXERCISE 2.2

1. How easy or difficult would it be for you to accept and not judge the following people? Tick the box that most closely reflects your viewpoint.

	Very easy	Easy	Difficult	Very difficult	Impossible
1. A mother who does not control her disruptive child whose behaviour prevents you from understanding the mother's story					
2. A man who does not follow your advice and complains about the same issues over and over again					
3. A patient who blames you for her troubles					
4. A man who refuses to take any responsibility for his health and wants you to tell him exactly what to do					
5. A patient who demands your help in an aggressive manner					
6. A patient who talks and talks, but not about his health					
7. A woman who keeps taking over the conversation and does not listen to you					

2. Look at the people you have ticked as 'difficult', 'very difficult' or 'impossible'. What are some of the reasons for these answers?

3. In what healthcare situations have you had to set aside personal biases, values and judgements?

EXERCISE 2.3

Read the following remarks made by patients who took part in a study on quality in general practice consultations in Glasgow, Scotland (Mercer *et al.*, 2007). Reflect on what you think the patients reacted to.

A. 'Some of them make you feel inadequate, you know you're getting old and you're getting senile and you're not able to take things in, I mean sometimes you feel that way, you feel as if oh I'll just lift my bag and jacket and go.'

B. 'I've got Dr X and Dr Y and the two of them have got totally different attitudes when it comes to talking to you, Dr X will take the time and listen to you.'

C. 'You feel as if you're taking up his [the doctor's] time . . . that makes you feel under pressure.'

D. 'When I go to see my doctor, I want him to see me, the person, not a bottle of methadone, I'm not that, I'm a person that's got needs and everything like everybody else, because I'm on methadone, I just don't get treated properly.'

EXERCISE 2.4

View the clips. These versions of the clips have the sound removed. Watch these silent versions then answer the following question.

In what ways are the practitioners' non-verbal approaches to the patients different?

EXERCISE 2.5

View the clip then answer the following question.

In what ways are the different aspects of connecting demonstrated in the clip? (The four aspects are: establishing rapport, accepting the patient as a person, effective non-verbal communication and allowing the patient to tell his or her story.)

MODULE 3: Assessing

View the clips then answer the following question.

In what ways do the healthcare practitioners show that they are attending/ listening?

EXERCISE 3.2

Twelve common behavioural barriers to listening are outlined following (McKay *et al.*, 2009). In what ways and under what circumstances might these barriers interfere with your listening?

1. *Comparing*: Comparing interferes with listening because you are constantly assessing which of you, for example, knows best. While a patient is talking, you are thinking, 'If you think that is hard, let me tell you how hard it actually can be.'

2. *Mind reading*: Mind reading pushes you to look for hidden meanings rather than to listen to what is actually being said. You might not completely trust that the patient is being open or honest about what they really want, so you shift your focus to possible hidden meanings through changes in intonation or facial expression.

3. *Rehearsing*: 'Rehearsing' means trying to look interested while you are planning and practising (rehearsing) your response.

4. *Filtering*: You often listen to some things and not others to avoid problems. For example, if you are afraid of confrontations, you will pay attention to what mood the patient is in. If you perceive no 'angry' signs, you will stop listening.

5. *Judging*: Judging is often done so quickly that you do not realise that you have done it. However, when you subconsciously label someone as being unintelligent or lazy, you tend to pay less attention to what they are saying.

6. *Dreaming*: The patient's words trigger your own associations and you begin to daydream. When you resume listening, you find the patient is talking about something else, leaving you with a gap in their story.

7. *Identifying*: Whatever the other person says triggers memories of similar experiences you have had, then, before you know it, you either interrupt the other person's flow to tell your story or start to think about your own experiences. Meanwhile, you stop paying attention to the other person's story.

8. *Advising*: You are keen to fix the patient's problems and are ready with advice, reassurance and suggestions after only hearing a few sentences. You like to start your reply with, 'If I were you, I would . . .' However, while searching for advice, you sometimes miss what the real problem is.

9. *Sparring*: Regardless of what the other person is saying, you start to look for issues to disagree and argue with them about. A common example is making sarcastic comments to dismiss the patient's point of view (the so-called put-down).

10. *Being right*: You go to great lengths to try to prove that you are right, thereby using tactics such as making up excuses, talking over the other person in a loud voice or distorting the truth.

11. *Derailing*: As soon as you feel out of your comfort zone or bored, you change the topic of the conversation, make a joke or banter to prevent any further discomfort. Meanwhile, you stop paying attention to the other person's story.

12. *Placating*: You want to please and be nice regardless of the situation. You say things like, 'of course you are', 'absolutely' and 'really', and find yourself unwittingly agreeing with everything the other person says.

EXERCISE 3.3

View the clips that show a mixture of verbal and non-verbal cues made by patients then answer the following questions.

1. What verbal and non-verbal cues do the patients give? What are the feelings that are revealed in the patients' voices or expressions?

2. Which cues do the practitioners pick up and which ones do they miss?

3. In what ways would you have dealt with the cues differently?

EXERCISE 3.4

The following clips are examples of different styles used by the same practitioner to obtain understanding of the whole person. View the clips and observe how the healthcare practitioner demonstrates a holistic approach.

EXERCISE 3.5

View the clip then answer the following question.

In what ways are the different aspects of assessing demonstrated in the clip? (The four aspects are: attending, sensitivity to patients' cues, understanding the whole person and asking questions.)

EXERCISE 3.5

MODULE 4: Responding

1. Think about how you would communicate to a patient that you care and compassionately relate to them.

2. View the following clips. In what ways do the practitioners show care and compassion?

EXERCISE 4.2

View the clips then answer the following question.

In what ways do the practitioners communicate that they are being positive?

EXERCISE 4.2

EXERCISE 4.3

The following clips show two different ways of giving information to the patient. View the clips then answer the following questions for each clip.

1. In what ways are the practitioners' approaches to giving information and explanations different?

2. In what ways do the patients react differently in response to the practitioners' explanations?

EXERCISE 4.4

Can you think of different reasons why you might use medical jargon?

EXERCISE 4.5

View the clip then answer the following question.

In what ways are the different aspects of responding demonstrated in the clip? (The four aspects are: demonstrating understanding, showing care and compassion, being positive, and giving relevant information and clear explanations.)

MODULE 5: Empowering

EXERCISE 5.1

1. What does 'empowerment' mean to you?

2. In what ways can you empower patients?

EXERCISE 5.2

1. What does 'self-management' mean to you?

2. Listen to the audio recording in which a healthcare professional talks about self-management. How do your answers to exercise 5.2, question 1 relate to the practitioner's view? You can read the transcript of the recording on self-management in Appendix 5 (p. 69).

EXERCISE 5.3

Watch the clips then answer the question that follows. The clips show different approaches to exploring with patients what they can do to improve their situation, identifying choices that are realistic for them and actively seeking their preferences.

In what ways do the practitioners differ in their approaches?

EXERCISE 5.4

View the clips then answer the question that follows.

In what ways do the healthcare practitioners foster the patients' beliefs in their own capabilities and competences?

EXERCISE 5.5

View the clip then answer the question that follows.

In what ways are the different aspects of empowering demonstrated in the clip? (The four aspects are: appreciating the bigger picture, helping patients to gain control, action-planning and confirming understanding, and confidence-building.)

MODULE 6: Putting it all together

EXERCISE 6.1

View the clips then answer the questions that follow.

1. Write down what components of the CARE Approach you think are happening at which time over the course of each encounter. You can use the blank graph to map this out by placing a cross against the component you think is occurring as each interaction moves along the time scale.

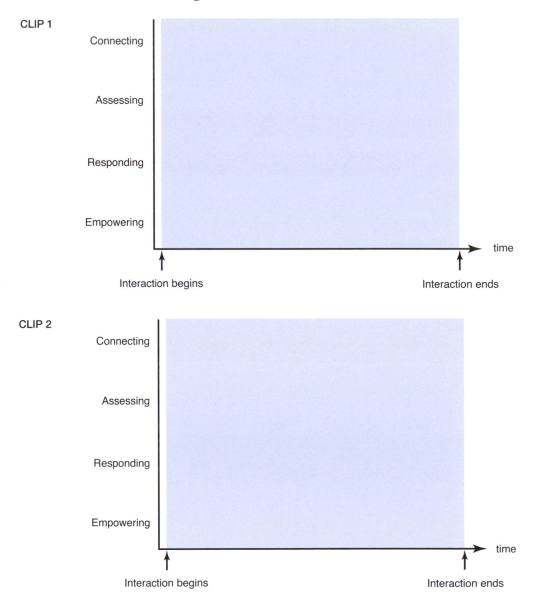

CLIP 3

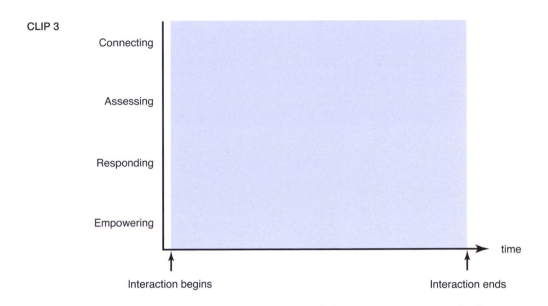

2. In what ways are the different components of the CARE Approach demonstrated in each clip?

EXERCISE 6.2

View the clips then answer the question that follows.

In what ways can the CARE Approach be applied to the way the patient is interacting with the healthcare professional?

EXERCISE 6.3

In what ways does the practitioner address the situation in the clip?

MODULE 7: The CARE Approach with colleagues and in teams

EXERCISE 7.1

1. What is your response to the terms 'team' and 'team working'? What thoughts come to mind? What feelings do you associate with these words?

2. Which teams, if any, do you consider yourself a member of at work?

3. Take one team that you belong to. What words would you use to describe this team?

EXERCISE 7.2

1. Think about the different ways you react to people in your team when they agree or disagree with you about an issue. Think about those who you trust highly and then those, who for a host of reasons, you do not trust greatly. When your team has to make important decisions, how important are levels of trust and agreement in achieving goals? For example, as a team leader, it can be a formative experience to have your ideas challenged by someone with whom you have a high level of trust. Similarly, if you are pushing for agreement in a climate of low trust, how sustainable are the changes or ideas you are promoting?

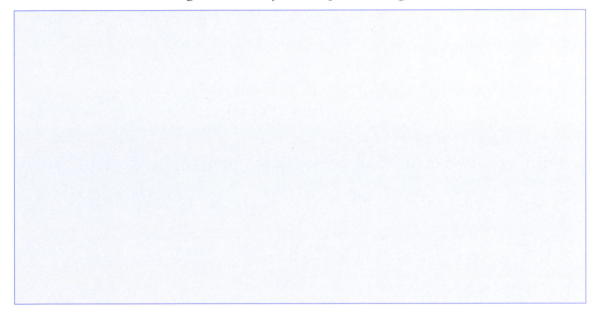

2. Think about a high-trust team or culture you have worked within. What helped to create that culture?

3. From your experience, in what ways can trust be broken and rebuilt within teams?

4. What is the level of trust like in your current team?

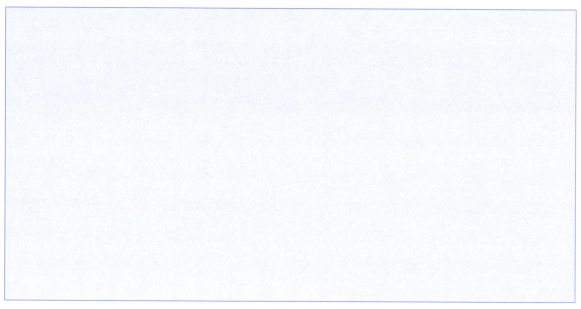

EXERCISE 7.3

For this exercise, work with a colleague and take turns answering the questions.

1. Quadrant 1: Identify one or more things in relation to your role that your colleagues already know (e.g. your patient caseload is very heavy, there is nowhere private to sit and have a coffee break).

2. Quadrant 3: Identify one or more things in relation to your role that your colleagues are not likely to know (e.g. you don't like your uniform, the time taken to travel to and from work, an aspect of your set of personal values that informs your practice, an aspect that you enjoy about your chosen profession).

3. Quadrant 2: Invite a colleague to say something about his/her perception of your role. This may be unknown to you. If a 'blind spot' is identified, how does this feel?

4. Reflect on how identifying such knowledge can affect the relative size of each of the quadrants.

EXERCISE 7.4

Think for a while about making change in the workplace – for example reorganising rotas or the office. How would that change affect a typical day for the people involved? Are there potential areas where conflicts or misunderstanding might arise?

EXERCISE 7.5

Reflect on each of the four dimensions of the CARE Approach in terms of your workplace. Use the following chart. If you feel comfortable doing so, you may wish to discuss your reflections with a colleague.

CARE Approach dimension	What it means to me in the workplace	What I already do to achieve this	What else I could do to achieve this
Connecting	(E.g. others showing a genuine interest in me as a person)	(E.g. make eye contact)	(E.g. let other's tell their story/point of view and try to avoid interrupting)
Assessing	(E.g. feeling heard and understood)	(E.g. pay attention to cues)	(E.g. pay attention to my barriers to listening)
Responding	(E.g. modifying responses to the circumstances that I encounter)	(E.g. check I have understood people correctly)	(E.g. consider that others may be right)
Empowering	(E.g. feeling trusted)	(E.g. I thank or acknowledge others)	(E.g. thank people and praise them when due)

POSSIBLE ANSWERS

MODULE 1: WHAT YOU BRING TO THE ENCOUNTER

Exercise 1.1

1. You might have responded with some/all of the following thoughts on 'caring: looking after someone, providing a service, showing respect, a way of relating to someone, a feeling and being emotionally involved.

In a recently published study (Pearcey, 2010) on people's views on caring, a group of nurses made the following statements:

- 'I think caring is about the way you are to people and the way you feel about people.'
- 'Caring is actually bothering to find out more about people and their problems – it's the bit that can make a difference.'
- 'Caring? It is the little things that we are not supposed to do any more.'

Exercise 1.3

1. You may have thought of things like: make time for me; focus on me; be respectful; being technically very competent; act in a way that shows I am in the right hands, being present and available to me; be interested in me as a person; not judge me; be sympathetic, friendly and approachable; empathic; trustworthy; intuitive; and/or explain how they can help me.
2. If they know and understand me, she or he is more likely to get my management right and make me confident that they want the best technical care possible for me. These qualities are common courtesy, show respect and signal that the doctor/nurse sees me as a person in my own right and not simply another patient.

MODULE 2: CONNECTING

Exercise 2.1

Non-verbally, all practitioners are focused on the patient and are not doing anything else that could indicate that they are distracted. They are facing the patient, leaning slightly forward and maintaining good eye contact. This creates the impression of openness and being interested.

Verbally, in Clip 1, the practitioner introduces herself by name and role and does not assume that the patient knows who she is. She checks how the patient would like to be addressed and says that she can be called by her first name as well – this is a personal touch that can help with connecting and putting the patient at ease. In Clip 2, the practitioner welcomes the patient by name and asks how she is. The practitioner responds in a friendly manner to the remark about the weather. In Clip 3, the practitioner thanks the patient for coming to the clinic. He addresses the patient by her first name and introduces himself as Dr Cotton.

Exercise 2.3

A. This remark relates to not feeling supported or involved in the encounter, because the GP has not taken on board the patient's level of understanding.
B. This is a remark concerning how being approached differently in terms of being given time and feeling listened to can make a difference.
C. This is a reaction to the GP's rushed attitude and how that relates to feelings of pressure.
D. This response relates to the perception of being judged by the GP and to feeling disrespected as a result.

Exercise 2.4

In Clip 1, the practitioner is oriented towards and looks at the patient. She makes supportive gesticulations, nods to encourage the patient to talk and seems generally calm and relaxed. The patient is clearly in distress and the practitioner comes across as approachable.

In Clip 2, the GP is slightly oriented towards the desk at the start. He shakes hands with the patient. He is focused on the patient. At the end of the clip, he has his hand over his mouth and folds his arms later on. This change in body language could create distance between him and the patient.

Exercise 2.5

Establishing rapport: The practitioner thanks the patient for coming along. She introduces herself by name and role and does not assume that the patient knows who she is (thereby prevents making the patient feel uncomfortable). She clarifies with the patient how she would like to be addressed and offers to be called by her first name as well, which adds a personal touch that can help with connecting and putting the patient at ease. Her approach seems engaging and is a good start for building rapport and trust.

Accepting the patient as a person: The practitioner comes across as approachable and gives the impression that she is genuinely interested in the patient.

Effective non-verbal communication: The practitioner's body language of facing the patient, maintaining good eye contact and leaning towards the patient signals that her focus is on the patient. She has a relaxed and friendly manner and her voice matches the content of what she says (her verbal communication).

Allowing the patient to tell his or her story: The practitioner lets the patient tell her story without interrupting and she shows signs of encouragement using non-verbal communication (such as nodding).

MODULE 3: ASSESSING

Exercise 3.1

In Clip 1, the practitioner shows that he is paying attention to the patient through his eye contact, the way in which he sits in his chair and by leaning forward. He does not rush the patient; instead, he gives the impression that the time is hers. He has an open and interested, non-judgemental expression on his face. He nods to encourage the patient to continue talking. He does not interrupt her, allows for silence and does not seem to feel the need to fill it. It looks like he pays close attention to her words as well as to her body language. His facial expressions are appropriate for the content of her story.

In Clip 2, the practitioner conveys that she is listening and paying attention by maintaining good eye contact. She nods to encourage the patient to keep talking and does not interrupt the patient. Her facial expressions are appropriate for the content of the patient's story.

Exercise 3.3

1. In Clip 1, the patient's facial expressions show that she is worried. Although she has been told in the past that everything is fine (with her toe), she is not convinced this is the case. In Clip 2, the patient looks down, her speech is broken and she speaks quietly. She gives the impression that she is feeling down and in a low mood. In Clip 3, the patient looks and verbalises that she is anxious and worried. Her facial expressions show that she is in distress.
2. In Clip 1, the practitioner appears to miss the patient's cue of being anxious about her toe and changes the topic. In Clip 2, the practitioner picks up on the patient's cue and asks her about her thoughts and feelings. Through this question, the patient is encouraged to open up about her experiences. By picking up on the cue, the patient can feel that the practitioner is genuinely interested and wanting to understand her story. In Clip 3, the practitioner does not address the patient's low mood or explore what the patient is anxious about. Instead, she changes the topic of conversation to investigations and to an activity that the patient would like to be able to do again.

Exercise 3.4

In Clip 1, the practitioner places the sleeping problem in a wider context. In Clip 2, the practitioner explores the home situation of the patient. In Clip 3, the practitioner picks up that the patient is looking tired. This leads to exploration of various aspects of the patient's life that contribute to the patient feeling exhausted. It is clear that the practitioner knows this patient quite well.

Exercise 3.5

Attending: The practitioner faces the patient, leans slightly forward, has good eye contact and is not doing anything else other than focusing on the patient.

Sensitivity to patients' cues: The patient is clearly in distress. The practitioner acknowledges the patient's feelings through an understanding attitude and allowing for silence.

Understanding the whole person and *asking questions*: The practitioner explores whether the patient has anyone to talk to and asks about the patient's daughter.

MODULE 4: RESPONDING

Exercise 4.1

1. You may have thought of things like: looking at them sympathetically, giving them a touch or allowing a silence, providing supportive responses in tune with the patient's state of mind.
2. In Clip 1, the practitioner makes empathic comments and normalises the patient's experiences of grief. In Clip 2, the practitioner makes reflective comments and validates the patient's experiences.

Exercise 4.2

In Clip 1, the practitioner summarises his understanding of the patient's story and feeds that back to her. Then he gives it a positive turn by talking about the possibility of changing the situation. He uses phrases like 'working together' and 'reversing things in the right direction'. His gestures and voice inflection match his verbal communication. In Clip 2, the practitioner is honest with the patient and offers alternatives to improve her situation.

Exercise 4.3

1. In Clip 1, the practitioner tailors his response carefully to the patient's level of understanding. His speech is precise and measured. He uses his non-verbal behaviour to engage with the patient. In Clip 2, the practitioner gives a detailed explanation about the patient's problem.
2. In Clip 1, the facial expressions of the patient and responses given by her indicate that she feels involved in the interaction. This enhances the process of connecting. In Clip 2, it is not possible to tell how much the patient feels involved in the interaction.

Exercise 4.4

Reasons you might use medical jargon include: familiarity with the jargon, not knowing other words, feeling intimidated by certain patients, being certain that patients know what you mean or being unaware that patients may not know the meaning, to validate yourself, lack of confidence or trying to impress, preventing patients from getting involved to save time and trying to hide that you do not know the answer to a patient's question.

Exercise 4.5

Demonstrating understanding: The practitioner puts the patient's experiences of tiredness in the wider context of her life.

Showing care and compassion: The practitioner offers supportive non-verbal responses in tune with the patient's state of mind.

Giving relevant information and clear explanations: The practitioner explains about the interaction of the tablets.

MODULE 5: EMPOWERING

Exercise 5.1

1. You may have said that 'empowerment' means: gaining control or mastery of something, being actively involved, having enhanced self-esteem, respect, enabling someone, to validate, making things possible, giving someone hope, feeling better, being more able to cope, and/or having increased confidence or independence.

2. You may have said that you can enable patients by: listening, giving tailored advice, enabling, helping people move on and/or making people feel better about themselves.

Exercise 5.3

In Clip 1, the patient says that she would like to go out more. The practitioner picks up on this and asks the patient whether she has any ideas about improving her situation. In Clip 2, the practitioner explains how she can facilitate the process of the patient's self-management through goal-setting.

Exercise 5.4

In Clip 1, the practitioner reinforces the need for the patient to lose weight and is positive and congratulatory. In Clip 2, the practitioner points out that the patient knows a lot and is doing well. In Clip 3 he congratulates the patient and points out the need to take time.

Exercise 5.5

Appreciating the bigger picture: The practitioner talks about the work situation and how that affects the patient's life.

Helping patients to gain control: The practitioner has a positive attitude and together he and the patient agree to do something about the patient's situation.

Action-planning and confirming understanding: In a calm and clear manner, the practitioner talks about the next steps. He also checks if the patient would like to talk about anything else.

MODULE 6: PUTTING IT ALL TOGETHER

Exercise 6.1

1.

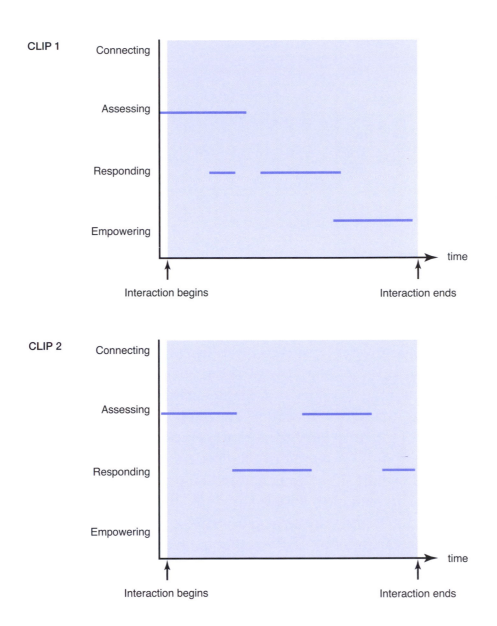

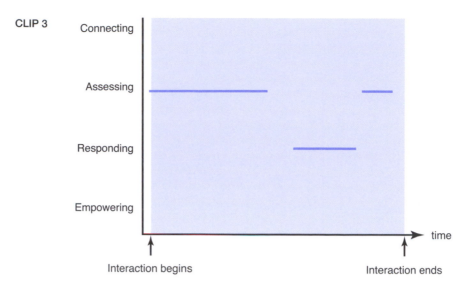

2. In Clip 1, the practitioner starts with assessing, he is attending and he asks the patient about her sister (understanding the whole person). He is responding, takes into account the patient's circumstances and is being positive. At the end of the encounter, he is empowering and is moving towards action-planning. Throughout the interaction, connecting seems to be going on. The practitioner's non-verbal communication matches the flow of the interaction and he approaches the patient in an accepting and non-intimidating manner. Clip 2 starts with assessing and then moves in and out of responding when the practitioner feeds back her understanding of the story. Further, she shows her involvement by reflecting back that she can see that it means a lot to the patient to go swimming with his son. Connecting seems part of the interaction. The practitioner has a friendly manner and allows the patient to tell his story. In Clip 3, the practitioner is mainly assessing. He listens and encourages the patient to tell his story (connecting). In a non-intrusive manner he asks whether the patient has received tablets from his friends (understanding the whole person). Then he moves into responding by briefly demonstrating his understanding of the story. At the end, he continues with assessing by asking a question. The practitioner seems accepting of the patient (connecting) throughout the encounter.

Exercise 6.2

Clip 1

Connecting: The patient focuses on the practitioner and moves slightly forward. He has a friendly manner, greets her and asks her how she is doing.

Assessing: The patient looks at the physiotherapist and gives the impression that he is concentrating on what she is saying.

Clip 2

Connecting/Assessing: The patient focuses on the practitioner when he speaks and her facial expressions and verbal utterances show that she is listening and in agreement with what the practitioner communicates.

   Responding: The patient seems very open and genuine in her responses.

Clip 3

Responding: The patient gives the impression that she is open and genuine in her response. She seems to have a good rapport with the practitioner.

Exercise 6.3

The practitioner reflects back to the patient his understanding of what is happening in their interaction. He acknowledges both viewpoints in a non-judgemental and non-intimidating manner.

References

- Arnold EC, Boggs KU. *Interpersonal Relationships: professional communication skills for nurses*. 5th ed. Philadelphia, PA: WB Saunders; 2007.
- Ashcroft L. Defusing 'Empowering': the what and the why. *Language Arts*. 1987; **64**(2): 142–56.
- Bandura A (ed.) *Self Efficacy in Changing Societies*. New York: Cambridge University Press; 1995.
- Batt-Rawden SA, Chisholm MS, Anton B, Flickinger TE. Teaching empathy to medical students: an updated systematic review. *Acad Med*. 2013; **88**(8): 1171–7
- Bikker AP, Mercer SW, Reilly D. A pilot prospective study on consultation and relational empathy, patient enablement, and health changes over 12 months in patients going to the Glasgow Homoeopathic hospital. *J Altern Complement Med*. 2005; **11**(4): 591–600.
- Bikker AP, Mercer SW, Cotton P. Connecting, Assessing, Responding, Empowering (CARE): a universal approach to person-centred, empathic healthcare encounters. *Educ Prim Care*. 2013; **23**(6): 454–7.
- Block P. *The Empowered Manager: positive political skills at work*. San Francisco, CA: Jossey-Bass; 1987.
- Borrill CS, Carletta J, Carter AJ, *et al.* (2001) *The Effectiveness of Health Care Teams in the National Health Service Report*. Available at: http://homepages.inf.ed.ac.uk/jeanc/DOH-final-report.pdf (accessed 9 December 2013).
- Brown JB, Stewart MA, Ryan BL. *Assessing Communication between Patients and Physicians: the measure of patient-centered communication*. Working paper series. Paper no. 95–2. 2nd ed. London, Ontario: Thames Valley Family Practice Research Unit and Centre for Studies in Family Medicine; 2001.
- Brown J, Lewis L, Ellis K, *et al.* Conflict on interprofessional primary health care teams – can it be resolved? *J Interprof Care*. 2011; **25**(1): 4–10.
- Campbell SM, Roland MO, Buetow S. Defining quality of care. *Soc Sci Med*. 2000; **51**: 1611–25.
- Cole SA, Bird J. *The Medical Interview: the three-function approach*. 2nd ed. St Louis, MO: Mosby; 2000.
- Davis CM. *Patient Practitioner Interaction: an experiential manual for developing the art of health care*. 4th ed. Thorofare, NJ: SLACK; 2006.
- Derksen F, Bensing J, Lagro-Janssen A. Effectiveness of empathy in general practice: a systematic review. *BJGP* 2013, **63**(606): 76–84.

- Dwamena F, Holmes-Rovner M, Gaulden C, *et al.* Interventions for providers to promote a patient-centred approach in clinical consultations. *Cochrane Database Syst Rev.* 2012; 12: CD003267. DOI: 10.1002/14651858.CD003267.pub2.
- Goffee R, Jones G. *Why Should Anyone Be Led by You? What it takes to be an authentic leader.* Boston, MA: Harvard Business School Press; 2006.
- Griffin S, Kinmonth A, Veltman M, *et al.* Effect on health-related outcomes of interventions to alter the interaction between patients and practitioners: a systematic review of trials. *Ann Fam Med.* 2004; **2**: 595–608.
- Hawkins J. *Wellbeing, Time Management, Self-Control and Self-Determination.* Available at: www.goodmedicine.org.uk/goodknowledge/wellbeing-time-management-self-control-self-determination (accessed 27 October 2013).
- Heywood S, Fitzgerald N, Winterbottom J. *Evaluation of Pilot Sites: the CARE approach and practice-based small group learning. A Report for NHS Education for Scotland.* Edinburgh: NHS Education for Scotland; 2012. A summary of the report is available at: www.nes.scot.nhs.uk/media/1574594/evaluation-of-care-pbsgl-short-summary.pdf (accessed 9 December 2013).
- Hojat M, Louis DZ, Markham FW, *et al.* Physicians' empathy and clinical outcomes for diabetic patients. *Acad Med.* 2011; **86**(3): 359–64.
- Hull M. *Consulting: communication skills for GPs in training* [DVD]. Birmingham: Royal College of General Practitioners Midland Faculty; 2005.
- Irving JA, Dobkin PL, Park J. Cultivating mindfulness in health care professionals: a review of empirical studies of mindfulness-based stress reduction (MBSR). *Complement Ther Clin Pract.* 2009; **15**(2): 60–8.
- Kabat-Zinn J. *Full Catastrophe Living.* 15th ed. London: Piatkus; 2004.
- Little P, Everitt H, Williamson I, *et al.* An observational study of the preferences of patients for the patient-centred approach to consultation in primary care. *BMJ.* 2000; **322**: 468–72.
- Little P, Everitt H, Williamson I, *et al.* An observational study of effect of patient centredness and positive approach on outcomes of general practice consultations. *BMJ.* 2001; **323**(7318): 908–11.
- Long Term Conditions Alliance Scotland (LTCAS), The Scottish Government. *'Gaun Yersel!': the self management strategy for long term conditions in Scotland.* Glasgow and Edinburgh: LTCAS and The Scottish Government; 2008. Available at: www.alliance-scotland.org.uk/download/library/lib_4e3ab5a3bfaec/ (accessed 27 October 2013).
- Luft J. *Group Processes: an introduction to group dynamics.* 3rd ed. Palto Alto, CA: Mayfield Publishing; 1984.
- McCabe C, Timmins F. *Communication Skills for Nursing Practice.* London: Palgrave McMillan; 2006.
- McCormack B, McCance T. *Person-Centred Nursing: theory and practice.* Oxford: Wiley-Blackwell; 2010.
- McKay M, Davis M, Fanning P. *Messages: the communication skills book.* 3rd ed. Oakland, CA: New Harbinger; 2009.

- Mead N, Bower P. Patient-centredness: a conceptual framework and review of the empirical literature. *Soc Sci Med.* 2000; **51**(7): 1087–110.
- Mercer SW, Reilly D, Watt GCM. The importance of empathy in the enablement of patients attending the Glasgow Homoeopathic Hospital. *Br J Gen Pract.* 2002; **52**(484): 901–5
- Mercer SW, Reynolds WJ. Empathy and quality of care. *Br J Gen Pract.* 2002; **52** Suppl.: S9–S12.
- Mercer SW, Maxwell M, Heaney D, *et al.* The consultation and relational empathy (CARE) measure: development and preliminary validation and reliability of an empathy-based consultation process measure. *Fam Pract.* 2004; **21**(6): 699–705.
- Mercer SW, McConnachie A, Maxwell M, *et al.* Relevance and practical use of the Consultation and Relational Empathy (CARE) Measure in general practice. *Fam Pract.* 2005; **22**(3): 328–34.
- Mercer SW, Cawston PG, Bikker AP. Quality in general practice consultations: a qualitative study of the views of patients living in an area of high socio-economic deprivation in Scotland. *BMC Fam Pract.* 2007; **8**: 22.
- Mercer SW, Neumann M, Wirtz M, *et al.* General practitioner empathy, patient enablement, and patient-reported outcomes in primary care in an area of high socio-economic deprivation in Scotland – a pilot prospective study using structural equation modeling. *Patient Educ Couns* 2008; **73**(2): 240–5.
- Mercer SW, Jani B, Wong SY, *et al.* Patient enablement requires physician empathy: a cross-sectional study of general practice consultations in areas of high and low socioeconomic deprivation in Scotland. *BMC Fam Pract.* 2012; **13**: 6.
- Neighbour R. *The Inner Consultation.* Lancaster: Kluwer Academic; 1987.
- Neumann M, Wirtz M, Bollschweiler E, *et al.* Determinants and patient-reported long-term outcomes of physician empathy in oncology: a structural equation modelling approach. *Patient Educ Couns.* 2007; **69**(1–3): 63–75.
- Neumann M, Bensing J, Mercer S, *et al.* Analyzing the 'nature' and 'specific effectiveness' of clinical empathy: a theoretical overview and contribution towards a theory-based research agenda. *Patient Educ Couns.* 2009; **74**: 339–46.
- Neumann M, Edelhauser F, Tauschel D, *et al.* Empathy decline and its reasons: a systematic review of studies with medical students and residents. *Acad Med.* 2011; **86**(8): 996–1009.
- Pearcey P. 'Caring? It's the little things we are not supposed to do anymore'. *Int J Nurs Pract.* 2010; **16**(1): 51–6.
- Platt FW, Gordon GH. *Field Guide to the Difficult Patient Interview.* Philadelphia, PA: Lippincott Williams & Wilkins; 1999.
- Powell, AE, Davies, Huw TO. The struggle to improve patient care in the face of professional boundaries. *Soc Sci Med.* 2012; **75**(6): 807–14.
- Rakel D, Barrett B, Zhang Z, *et al.* Perception of empathy in the therapeutic encounter: effects on the common cold. *Patient Educ Couns.* 2011; **85**(3): 390–7.

- Reynolds W. *The Measurement and Development of Empathy in Nursing.* Aldershot: Ashgate; 2000.
- Riess H, Kelley JM, Bailey RW, *et al.* Empathy training for resident physicians: a randomized controlled trial of a neuroscience-informed curriculum. *J Gen Intern Med.* 2012; **27**(10): 1280–6.
- Salas E, DiazGranados D, Weaver SJ, *et al.* Does team training work? Principles for health care. *Acad Emerg Med.* 2008; **15**(11): 1002–9.
- Scottish Government, The. *The Healthcare Quality Strategy for NHS Scotland.* Edinburgh: The Scottish Government; 2010. Available at: www.scotland.gov.uk/Resource/Doc/311667/0098354.pdf (accessed 27 October 2013).
- Spreitzer GM. Social structural characteristics of psychological empowerment. *Acad Manage J.* 1996; **39**(2): 483–504.
- Spreitzer GM. Taking stock: a review of more than twenty years of research on empowerment at work. In: Barling J, Cooper CL, editors. *The SAGE Handbook of Organizational Behavior. Vol. 1: Micro Perspectives.* London, Thousand Oaks, CA, New Delhi and Singapore: SAGE; 2008. pp. 54–72.
- Stewart M, Brown JB, Weston WW, *et al. Patient-Centered Medicine: transforming the clinical method.* 3rd ed. London: Radcliffe Publishing; 2014.
- Thomas KW, Kilmann RH. *Thomas-Kilmann Conflict Mode Instrument.* Mountain View, CA: CPP; 2007 (1974).
- Wensing M, Jung HP, Mainz J, *et al.* A systematic review of the literature on patient priorities for general practice care. Part 1: description of the research domain. *Soc Sci Med.* 1998; **47**: 1573–88.
- Xyrichis A, Lowton K. What fosters or prevents interprofessional teamworking in primary and community care? A literature review. *Int J Nurs Stud.* 2008; **45**: 140–53.

CPD with Radcliffe

You can now use a selection of our books to achieve CPD (Continuing Professional Development) points through directed reading.

We provide a free online form and downloadable certificate for your appraisal portfolio. Look for the CPD logo and register with us at: www.radcliffehealth.com/cpd